GLOBETROTTER™

Travel Guide

TOKYO

D1827521

SUE THOMPSON

NEW HOLLAND

NEW
HOLLAND

★★★ Highly recommended
★★ Recommended
★ See if you can

First published in 2004
by New Holland Publishers (UK) Ltd
London • Cape Town • Sydney • Auckland
10 9 8 7 6 5 4 3 2 1

website: www.newhollandpublishers.com

Garfield House, 86 Edgware Road
London W2 2EA, United Kingdom

80 McKenzie Street, Cape Town,
8001, South Africa

14 Aquatic Drive, Frenchs Forest,
NSW 2086, Australia

218 Lake Road, Northcote,
Auckland, New Zealand

Distributed in the USA by
The Globe Pequot Press, Connecticut

Keep us Current
Information in travel guides is apt to change, which is
why we regularly update our guides. We'd be grateful
to receive feedback if you've noted something we
should include in our updates. If you have new
information, please share it with us by writing to the
Publishing Manager, Globetrotter, at the office nearest
to you (addresses on this page). The most significant
contribution to each new edition will receive a free
copy of the updated guide.

Publishing Manager (UK): Simon Pooley
Publishing Manager (SA): Thea Grobbelaar
DTP Cartographic Manager: Genené Hart
Editor: Melany McCallum
Design and DTP: Lellyn Creamer
Picture Researcher: Shavonne Johannes
Cartographer: Nicole Engeler
Consultant: Nigel Hicks
Proofreader: Claudia Dos Santos

Reproduction by Hirt & Carter (Pty) Ltd, Cape Town
Printed and bound in Hong Kong by Sing Cheong
Printing Co. Ltd

Photographic Credits:
Jeroen Snijders: pages 11, 14, 20, 24, 25, 27, 59, 66, 76,
85, 86; **Jon Arnold Images/Demetrio Carrasco:** pages 4,
50; **Jon Arnold Images/James Montgomery:** pages 15,
53, 108; **Jon Arnold Images/R Butcher:** pages 94, 99;
Jon Arnold Images/Walter Bibikow: page 56; **Neil
Setchfield:** pages 19, 60, 63; **Sue Thompson:** cover,
pages 8, 18, 21, 22, 26, 30, 33, 36, 37, 43, 47, 48, 62, 64,
67, 68, 70, 72, 73, 74, 77, 78, 81, 82, 83, 84, 88, 89, 90,
91, 93, 95, 96, 98, 100, 103, 104, 105, 106, 110 113, 114;
Sylvia Cordaiy Photo Library/Ian Leonard: pages 6, 7,
9, 12, 16, 23, 28, 29, 34, 41, 42, 46, 52, 55; **Sylvia
Cordaiy Photo Library/Claire Stout:** title page.

Front Cover: *The Edo-Period temple, Meguro Fudo-son.*
Title Page: *Awa Odora dancers.*

CONTENTS

1
Introducing Tokyo

Once a 17th-century **fishing village**, Tokyo now ranks with Mexico City and São Paulo as one of the world's biggest **urban conglomerations**. Burned to ashes on numerous occasions, flattened by the Great Kantō Earthquake of 1923 and **carpet-bombed** by the Allied forces in 1945, this huge Japanese metropolis has risen time and time again. At its heart lies the **Imperial Palace**, haughty and aloof; beyond sprawls an eye-searing urban jungle teeming with world-class shops, showcase architecture, restaurants and museums. From avant-garde to retro, from chic to tacky, Tokyo does nothing by halves.

This book takes you clockwise around the circular Yamanote Line from **Imperial Tokyo** to **Old Tokyo**, beneath the cherry blossoms of Ueno, Yanaka and Asakusa. It continues through the department stores and museums of Marunouchi and Ginza, to **Cool Tokyo** in the shops, restaurants and bars of Ebisu, Shibuya and Harajuku via **Virtual Tokyo**, the futuristic city out in Tokyo Bay. Journey's end is among the skyscrapers of Shinjuku and the byways of Ikebukuro and Sugamo. Trains run on time, crime is low and people are generally helpful, so stay cool and go with the flow.

Outside Tokyo there are a number of compelling day or weekend excursions, including the port of Yokohama and the medieval temple town of Kamakura. Further afield lies Hakone in the shadow of Mount Fuji, Japan's ultimate icon, and Nikkō, home to the grand mausoleum of Tokugawa Ieyasu, the *shōgun* who first made Tokyo his capital in 1603.

TOP ATTRACTIONS

*** **Asakusa and Yanaka:** a taste of Old Tokyo.
*** **Meiji Jingu and Harajuku:** from Shinto to shopping.
*** **Tokyo National Museum:** dazzling 7th-century Hōryū-ji treasures.
*** **Shinjuku:** from skyscrapers to low life.
*** **Tokyo Bay:** architecture for the 21st century.
*** **Kamakura:** 13th-century temple town.
*** **Tsukiji Fish Market:** tuna capital of the world.

Opposite: *A young woman in a traditional kimono on Coming-of-Age Day.*

Opposite: *Boats along the Sumida River recall the days when canals were the capital's main transport arteries.*
Below: *The top of Ebisu Garden Place Tower offers good restaurants and one of Tokyo's best free views.*

THE LAND

On a similar latitude to Cyprus and Los Angeles, Tokyo sprawls over the Kantō Plain of Honshū. **Central Tokyo** is defined as the city's 23 *ku* (wards). **Tokyo Metropolis** includes Central Tokyo, the Tama district to the west, and the Izu and Ogasawara Islands, whereas the **Greater Tokyo Metropolitan Area** adds in the surrounding prefectures of Saitama, Kanagawa and Chiba, and the cities of Kawasaki and Yokohama. The **National Capital Region** consists of Tokyo Metropolis and its seven surrounding prefectures, an area of 40 million people.

Tokyo has been the political, financial, administrative and commercial capital of Japan since 1868, when its name was changed from **Edo** (Inlet) to Tokyo (Eastern Capital). As the old name suggests, water has played a crucial part in the city's development: the Edo, Sumida and Ara rivers of the Kantō Plain all flow out to the sea through Tokyo.

Topography

Like Rome, Tokyo too is built on seven hills, only less obviously so. The **Musashino Plateau**, formed from volcanic ash emitted by Mount Fuji long ago, gives rise to seven areas of highlands in the west of the city known traditionally as *yamanote* (high city), while to the east lies *shitamachi* (low city), an area of waterways and flatlands.

Destruction by fire, earthquake and bombing in the first half of the 20th century, followed by relentless building and land reclamation have now blurred the distinct topographical boundaries of the Edo Period (1600–1868). Nevertheless, walking up and down the slopes of areas such as Akasaka and Yanaka today is still sufficient reminder that Tokyo is far from flat.

Growth of the City

Tokyo may appear to have
sprawled at random over the centuries, but its basic building blocks
are still intact. Four hundred years
ago, when the entire city virtually
fitted into the area encircled by
today's Yamanote Line, the heart
of Edo was the *shōgun's* **castle** in
the grounds now occupied by the
Imperial Palace.

Major roads such as Mejiro-dōri and Hongō-dōri
(then the Nakasendō) also denote a continuity with the
past. So do the temples of Sensō-ji (Asakusa), Kanei-ji
(Ueno) and Zōjō-ji (Shiba), designated in the 17th century to guard the city. However, even a citizen of the
Meiji Period (1868–1912) would now find the extent
of the city overwhelming: old post stations such as
Shinjuku and Shinagawa (outside the 15 wards that
comprised Tokyo before 1889) are now **satellite cities**
in their own right, as are Shibuya and Ikebukuro.

Population Growth

By the early 18th century, Edo had mushroomed into the
world's biggest metropolis with a population of around
1.2 million inhabitants. The majority lived in *shitamachi*,
but in the 1880s growth began to shift toward the high
city. By 1935 Tokyo had 6.4 million inhabitants (on a par
with London and New York), a figure which plunged to
3.5 million in the aftermath of Allied bombing raids in
1945. Growth, however, resumed with a vengeance
after World War II.

A City of Waterways

For centuries, Tokyo's
waterways provided its main
routes of transportation as
well as the location of its rice
warehouses and markets.
Far-fetched though it seems
today, the **Sumida River**
was Tokyo's equivalent of
the **Grand Canal** in Venice.
In the Meiji Period (1868–
1912), the advent of the
omnibus, the rickshaw and
the railway led to the decline
of the canals, which also
increasingly disappeared
under landfill as the city
expanded. Like London, however, Tokyo found renewed
interest in developing its
waterfront in the late 20th
century. Tokyo Bay is now at
the cutting edge of modern
Japanese architecture.

Climate

Japan has **very distinct
seasons** and **huge temper-
ature extremes** owing to
its proximity to the eastern
seaboard of the Asian
landmass, which subjects

TOKYO	J	F	M	A	M	J	J	A	S	O	N	D
AVERAGE TEMP. °F	41	43	48	57	66	72	77	81	73	64	55	46
AVERAGE TEMP. °C	5	6	9	14	19	22	25	27	23	18	13	8
HOURS OF SUN DAILY	6	5	5	5	6	4	5	6	4	4	4	5
RAINFALL in	2	2	4	5	5	7	5	6	7	6	4	2
RAINFALL mm	45	60	100	125	138	185	126	148	180	164	89	46
DAYS OF RAINFALL	2	5	14	10	6	11	13	10	8	6	7	2

Right: *Koishikawa Shokubutsu-en in spring, when Japan's 400 varieties of cherry tree come into bloom.*

Opposite: *Even the birds appreciate Ueno Park, one of the capital's largest green spaces.*

the archipelago to the cold northwesterly monsoon in winter and, in summer, to the warm moist air of the southeasterly monsoon. Tokyo escapes the worst of the extremes, apart from summer, when **humidity** rises during the *tsuyu* (rainy season) that prevails from June to mid-July. In August, temperatures often soar to unpleasantly sticky levels of over 30°C (86°F).

Winters tend to be cold and crisp, but often sunny; snow is rare. Spring and autumn are both pleasant and the most popular times for visiting Japan to see the cherry blossoms and autumn leaves respectively. The **typhoon season** lasts from September to October, though most typhoons tend to blow themselves out well before they reach Tokyo.

Flora and Fauna

Tokyo is hardly mainstream bird-watching territory, yet it is home to more birds than one might think, particularly to waterfowl, which enjoy the city's many ponds and gardens. The Japanese love of nature also means that Tokyo has several 'official' natural symbols: its official bird is the **yurikamome** (the black-headed gull, after which the Tokyo Bay monorail is named); its official tree is the **ginkgo**, which has fan-shaped leaves (and lines many of Tokyo's pavements) and its official flower is the **Somei-Yoshino cherry blossom**.

Environment

In the 1960s Tokyo was one of the most polluted cities on earth, the air thick with industrial fumes from coal-fired power stations. Switching from coal to oil in the 1970s helped improve the situation. Now, Japan has some of the strictest automobile emission standards in the world, though it still has a long way to go in cleaning up decades of industrial toxic waste. Tokyo traffic is invariably slow-moving, which is why rail and subway are the best way to get around. Noise is endemic: piped music, strident political campaigning via megaphone and taped announcements are just some of Tokyo's aural hazards.

Earthquakes

Japan sits uncomfortably at the junction of three major **tectonic plates**: the Eurasian plate to the west, the Philippine plate to the south and the Pacific plate to the east. Off the eastern edge of the archipelago, where these plates collide, is a series of **marine trenches** plunging to depths of 9000m (30,000ft). As a result Japan is a permanent hot bed of **volcanic and seismic activity**. Around 60 volcanoes are now classified as active, among them Mount Fuji – even though it has not erupted since 1707.

WHAT TO DO IN AN EARTHQUAKE
• Switch off gas supply and all electrical appliances. • Open all the doors to prevent jamming. • Stay away from glass/heavy objects. Preferably stand in a ground floor doorway or crouch under a table. • At night, have a torch to hand. Know the location of emergency exits in your hotel. • When the tremors have died down go to the nearest open space/designated emergency centre. • If in a car, stop immediately. Switch off engine and try to take shelter. • Get in touch with your embassy as soon as possible.

The most devastating quake in the past 100 years was the **Great Kantō Earthquake**, which struck Tokyo and Yokohama at 11:58 on 1 September 1923. Registering an estimated 7.9 on the Richter scale, the quake sparked fires that did much more damage than the seismic activity itself. Seventy-five per cent of Tokyo's buildings were damaged or destroyed and around 140,000 people were reported dead or missing.

HISTORY IN BRIEF
Capitals of Japan before Tokyo

Japanese civilization spread from west to east. From the 8th to the 12th centuries the imperial capitals of **Nara** (710–794) and **Kyoto** (794–1185) shaped Japan's political, cultural and religious landscape as depicted in the *The Tale of Genji*, a voluminous novel written around AD1000 by Murasaki Shikibu, a lady courtier who describes a rarified world of gorgeous costumes and poetry contests.

By the late 12th century the rise of military clans led to the eclipse of the imperial family. In 1185, the warrior Minamoto Yoritomo established his capital at **Kamakura**, when present-day Tokyo scarcely figured on the map. The Ashikaga dynasty, which succeeded the Minamotos, moved the capital back to Kyoto in the 14th century, but eventually faded from power. After an era of civil war, three warlords gradually drew Japan back under centralized control. The final victor, **Tokugawa Ieyasu** (1543–1616) chose the small inlet of **Edo** as his capital.

Edo before 1600

The first castle at Edo was built in 1457 by **Ōta Dōkan**, a feudal lord famed for holding poetry contests in the citadel's vast fortifications. It was on this site in the early 17th century that **Tokugawa Ieyasu** built his castle and where the **Imperial Palace** now stands. Early on, Ieyasu invited fishermen from western Japan to the tiny hamlet of Edo in order to supply the castle with fish (*see* page 66).

Edo Period (1600–1868)

As victor of the **Battle of Sekigahara** in 1600, Ieyasu was declared *shōgun* in 1603. To retain the loyalty of his feudal lords (*daimyō*) and drain them of surplus cash that might fuel rebellion, Ieyasu instituted a system requiring them to spend 6–12 months at a time in Edo. *Daimyō* attended by armies of servants and aides travelling the main highways into Edo became a familiar sight. Ultimately, this succession of traffic fuelled the new capital's explosive growth.

Opposite: *Most Japanese schoolgirls wear uniform and knee-length socks.*

Edo Castle was completed in 1640, long after Ieyasu's death, but from its early days it served as the focal point of the city's development. The *daimyō* closest to the Tokugawa family built their residences directly around the inner moat; those less closely linked built beyond.

HISTORICAL CALENDAR

1457 The first castle is erected at Edo.
1603 *Shōgun* Tokugawa Ieyasu establishes his capital at Edo.
1639 'Closed country' policy adopted.
1657 Great Meireki Fire kills 100,000.
1853 Commodore Perry arrives at Uraga Bay.
1868 Power is restored to the Meiji Emperor.
Edo becomes Tokyo, capital of Japan.
1872 Inauguration of the Yokohama-Shimbashi railway.

1905 Japan wins the Russo-Japanese War.
1923 Great Kantō Earthquake kills over 100,000.
1925 JR Yamanote Line opens.
1926 Emperor Hirohito ascends throne; Shōwa era begins.
1941 Japan bombs Pearl Harbor.
1945 Allied bombing raids devastate Tokyo. Japan surrenders after the atomic bombings of Hiroshima and Nagasaki.
1945–52 Allied occupation of Japan.
1964 Tokyo hosts the Olympic Games.

1989 Emperor Hirohito dies and the Heisei era begins. Nikkei Stock Index reaches all-time high.
1991 Tokyo Metropolitan Government Building opened in Shinjuku. Bubble economy deflates.
1995 Aum Shinrikyō sarin gas attack on Tokyo subway.
1999 Ishihara Shintarō is elected Governor of Tokyo.
2000 Koizumi Junichiro becomes the prime minister, promising radical reform.
2002 Japan and South Korea host the FIFA World Cup.

Above: *Ginza's boulevards stretch far and wide at the Sukiyabashi intersection.*

COMMODORE MATTHEW PERRY (1794–1858)

On 8 July 1853 a US naval officer called Commodore Perry sailed a fleet of four 'black ships' into Tokyo Bay, carrying demands from the American President for Japan to open its ports and give better treatment to foreign shipwrecked sailors. This proved the beginning of the end of Japan's self-imposed isolation, which had commenced in 1639, when Charles I was King of England. In 1854 Perry returned to hear the response to his demands, which resulted in the signing of the **Kanagawa Treaty** and the opening in 1858 of the port of Yokohama.

Both categories, however, lived in the *yamanote*. To service the needs of the *daimyō*, a growing army of labourers and artisans flocked to Edo, where they took up residence in the *shitamachi* east of the castle around Nihombashi.

Reflecting this topographical hierarchy, society came to be strictly divided into four classes: the **samurai** (warrior), the **farmer**, the **artisan** and the **merchant**. 'Unclean castes' such as tanners and butchers ossified into the *burakumin* ethnic minority that still exists today. The introspective nature of Japanese society was reinforced in 1639 when a Christian uprising prompted the third *shōgun*, **Tokugawa Iemitsu**, to close the country. For the next two centuries Japan's sole contact with Western science and knowledge was via the Dutch trading post at **Dejima** in Nagasaki on Kyūshū.

As merchants gathered untold wealth, Edo and other **castle towns** such as Ōsaka, Nagoya and Kanazawa grew into thriving **commercial centres**, though natural disasters frequently brought home the uncertainty of life, particularly the **Great Meireki Fire** of 1657, which decimated over half of Edo's buildings, damaged the castle and killed 100,000 people. Between fires, earthquakes and other calamities, citizens chose a hedonistic approach to life: the greatest period in *shitamachi* urban culture was the Genroku era (1688–1703), when the *kabuki* (*see* page 64) and *bunraku* (puppet) theatres flourished, and wood-block prints known as *ukiyo-e* (floating world pictures) became all the rage.

As the 18th century progressed, rice riots, economic strains and the effects of self-imposed isolation began to tell. In the first half of the 19th century, Western maritime expansion brought foreign ships to Japan's coastline, but only when **Commodore Perry** arrived in 1853 did Japan's closed-door policy begin to crumble. The end came in 1868, when an alliance of feudal domains in Kyūshū successfully wiped out 700 years of military rule in the name of the young Emperor Meiji.

Meiji Period (1868–1912)

In 1868 Edo was formally renamed Tokyo (Eastern Capital) and the imperial family moved from Kyoto into Edo Castle. Feudalism was gradually dismantled and the **Meiji Constitution** came into effect in 1890. Starved of outside contact for so long, the Japanese began to gorge on Western culture and knowledge: out went samurai topknots and kimono and in came bowler hats and long skirts. New institutions such as public parks, department stores and music halls made their debut; so did the rickshaw, the first steam locomotive (which started running between Shimbashi and Yokohama in 1872) and the horse-drawn trolley, in 1883.

Architecture, too, saw new developments, particularly in the **Ginza** district, which after being burned to the ground by fire in 1872 was rebuilt in chic, foreign **brick**. Always unpopular with local residents, who found the houses expensive and impractical, this brick town was eventually pulverized by the Great Kantō Earthquake of 1923.

Meiji Japan also saw the rise of the **zaibatsu**, industrial conglomerates controlled by families such as the Mitsubishi and Sumitomo. **Marunouchi** emerged as the business district east of the Imperial Palace, and **Nagatachō** and **Kasumigaseki** as the new political and bureaucratic centres to the west.

Now too, a growing sense of national confidence backed by the tangible benefits of newly obtained Western science prompted military expansion overseas: as the victor of the **Sino-Japanese War** in 1895, Japan assumed control of Taiwan; subsequent to the Russo-Japanese War (1905) it also took Sakhalin and Manchuria, followed in 1910 by Korea.

RAILROAD TRIVIA

On arriving in Yokohama in 1878, the intrepid Victorian traveller Isabella Bird (1831–1904) took the 29km (18-mile) Tokyo railroad, completed in 1872. Then, first-class carriages were fitted with 'deeply-cushioned red morocco seats' but carried very few passengers. At Shimbashi Station, Bird describes disembarking alongside 200 Japanese producing a combined clatter of 400 clogs. Now, JR East carries a daily average of 16.5 million passengers on more than 7360km (4600 miles) of track. The **Yamanote Line** alone carries 87,000 passengers per hour, running one train every two and a half minutes.

JAPANESE NAMES

The Japanese give their surname first, followed by their given name, a practice used throughout this book. So, Mishima (surname) Yukio is how the Japanese refer to this well-known author, even though translations of Mishima's work use the reverse order (Yukio Mishima) to conform to Western practice. When addressing a Japanese person add 'San' to the surname, e.g. Suzuki San: Mr, Mrs, or Miss Suzuki.

Taishō Period (1912–26)

The death of the Emperor Meiji ushered in a new, less monumental era, symbolized by the mental frailty of the new emperor. Although World War I was a physically distant affair from Japan's perspective, the Japanese economy benefited from providing munitions to the allies. Ensuing inflation, however, caused rice riots in 1918. A brief flirtation with **democracy** followed, which ended in 1921 with the assassination of Prime Minister Hara Takashi by a right-wing fanatic.

The new **intellectual** preoccupations of the Taishō Period are still tangible in a stroll through the bookshops of Jimbochō, though in the Roaring Twenties it was to **Ginza** and Asakusa that the *moba* and *moga* (modern boy and modern girl) gravitated for fun. The new, willowy, wistful look of the Taishō era was epitomized in the art of Takehisa Yumeiji. In 1923 the music came to a stop with the Great Kantō Earthquake, which devastated Tokyo. Worldwide depression followed after 1929, ushering in a decade of fear ahead of World War II.

Shōwa Period (1926–89)

Largely rebuilt by 1930, Tokyo resumed its relentless spread across satellite areas such as Shinjuku and Ikebukuro, mirroring the Japanese army's invasion of China in 1937 and Southeast Asia in 1942. Yet, in 1945 Tokyo was again razed to the ground, this time by Allied bombing raids (*see* opposite panel).

Under the **Allied Occupation** (1945–52), Tokyo rose once more, aided by the outbreak of the **Korean War** in 1950, which boosted Japan's heavy industry and therefore economic growth. The **Tokyo 1964 Olympics** and the opening of the first **Shinkansen (bullet train)** line that year marked Japan's return to international respectabili-ty, but did little to mask

Opposite: *The Shinkansen ('bullet train') has a top speed of 300kph (188mph).* **Below:** *The Japanese are among the world's most avid readers of books and magazines.*

the social volatility of the 1960s, which began with protests against the renewal of the United States Security Treaty (Anpo) and ended with anti-Vietnam demonstrations that paralyzed Tokyo University.

Tokyo was now facing a growing **urban nightmare**: too little housing, too much uncontrolled construction, too much traffic and the worst pollution since the early 19th century, caused by the heavy use of coal. Pollution-related illnesses rocketed before measures to control industrial emissions in the 1970s brought some improvement. Like the new skyscrapers in Shinjuku, inflation soared after the 1973 oil shock, but Japan coped and growth resumed.

By the early 1980s Japan had amassed a huge **trade surplus** with the US and Europe. At the **Plaza Accord** of 1985, G7 member countries decided to orchestrate a rise in the yen in order to make Japan export less and import more. The yen obliged by doubling in value from ¥250 to ¥121 relative to the US$ by the end of 1987, which alleviated the trade surplus for a while. To slow the yen's rise, however, the government slashed interest rates, inadvertently paving the way for a **speculative boom** in property, golf-club memberships, paintings and fine wines.

THE NIGHT TOKYO BURNED

During 1945 sixty-six Japanese cities were heavily bombed by the Allied forces. In the closing stages of World War II, Tokyo was bombed over 100 times. No single raid, however, caused more damage than that of the night of **9–10 March 1945**, when a host of B-29 bombers took to the air and dropped M-69 incendiary devices over the low city, principally Asakusa, Fukagawa, Honjō and Nihombashi. In the ensuing wall of flame, 25 per cent of the city's buildings were destroyed, one million people were made homeless and over 100,000 were killed or injured.

Above: The Marunouchi business district by the Imperial Palace developed in the late 19th century.

In a capital awash with cash, the **value of land** began to soar as banks encouraged individuals and businesses to borrow cheaply against the value of increasingly **inflated assets**. Despite the death of Emperor Hirohito in January 1989, the Nikkei stock market index carried onwards and upwards to an all-time high of 38,915. The stratosphere – or so it seemed – was the limit.

Heisei Period (1989~)

By 1992 the Tokyo Metropolitan Government had moved into its new skyscrapers in Shinjuku, but the stock market bubble had already burst. Now land prices too began to plummet. The Japanese **miracle** turned into a **nightmare**. Financial sector profits collapsed under the weight of bad debts and **bankruptcies** rumbled on throughout the 1990s. Unemployment soared to nearly five per cent. For the first time, cardboard cities in Ueno and Shinjuku became part of Tokyo's landscape; consumers lost the urge to splurge and began piling into budget coffee shops and ¥100 stores rather than the grandest of Ginza department stores. Unfortunately, the pain is still far from over.

In 1999 Tokyoites voted in as their governor **Ishikawa Shintarō**, a right-wing nationalist strongly opposed to government intervention in the running of Tokyo.

GOVERNMENT AND ECONOMY

Tokyo is the seat of both the **national government** and the **Tokyo Metropolitan Government** (**TMG**), which administers Tokyo Metropolis from its sky-scraper headquarters in Shinjuku.

REIGN NAMES

In Japan, each emperor has a specific era or reign name. Emperor Hirohito, who came to the throne in 1926, presided over the **Shōwa** (Enlightened Peace) era (not, as it turns out, the most appropriate of name choices). His son, Emperor Akihito, who acceded in 1989, rules under the name **Heisei** (Accomplished Peace). The year of imperial accession marks the first year of the reign name (i.e. Heisei 1 = 1989). To calculate Japanese reign names, subtract the year before accession (e.g. 1925 or 1988) from the current year of the Western calendar. Thus 1980 = Shōwa 55 and 2004 = Heisei 16.

f **Japan** adopted on 3 May 1947,
ational monarchy (which desig-
symbol of state and of the unity
ish-style **parliamentary polit-
Diet**. The post-war constitution
gn right to war and enshrines
the rights of the people, the separation of religion and
state and an independent judicial framework based on
a **Supreme Court**. The Diet is the highest organ of state
and consists of the **House of Representatives** (the lower
chamber) with 480 members elected to four-year terms,
and the **House of Councillors** (the upper chamber) with
252 members elected to six-year terms. Executive power
resides with the **cabinet**, which answers to the Diet. The
prime minister is appointed on the recommendation of
the Diet by the emperor. National institutions such as the
Diet Building (Kokkaigiji-dō), the Supreme Court and
the **Bank of Japan** are all Tokyo landmarks.

Japan's **civil service** is an elite body of mostly Tokyo
University graduates that staff the Prime Minister's
Office and government ministries. In effect, the Bank
of Japan, the Ministry of Finance (MOF) and the Ministry
of Energy, Trade and Industry (METI) rule the economy.

In 1990 the Diet mooted the idea of moving national
legislative, administrative and judicial functions out of
Tokyo to a **new capital** in order to alleviate excessive
pressure on the National Capital Region and to avoid
total administrative paralysis in the event of a devastating earthquake.

Tokyo Metropolitan Government

The TMG, which administers
the 23 *ku* area as well as 26
cities, five towns and eight vil-
lages, is strongly opposed to
any move to relocate the capital,
estimating that the cost could be
as high as US$150 billion.

AN AGEING SOCIETY

One of Japan's biggest
problems is the rapid rate at
which its society is ageing.
By 2020 nearly 27 per cent
of the population will be over
65, compared to just 16 per
cent in the USA and 18 per
cent in the UK. Life expect-
ancy in Japan is now nearly
85 for women and 78 for
men, yet the birth rate is
dropping. The population is
expected to peak between
2005 and 2007. Funding
the cost of the elderly is
already proving a strain on
public finances.

Below: *Japan's flag is
called the* Hi no Maru,
literally 'Circle of the Sun'.

A SEA OF DEBT

A legacy of indiscriminate lending in the bubble era of the 1980s has left Japan's banking system with a headache of monumental proportions caused by four recessions since 1990. Estimates of bad loans range from US$300 billion to US$1.3 trillion. National debt too is astronomical, standing at 140 per cent of GDP. Yet, interest rates have been at or close to zero for nearly 10 years now and consumer prices have fallen over the same period. Though some of the benefit has come through in the form of lower prices, restructuring of the economy remains a pressing political concern.

Opposite: *Thousands of commuters make their way to their local train stations every day.*
Below: *The Bank of Japan's mission is to ensure the country's financial stability.*

The TMG is headed by the Governor of Tokyo, who is elected by the people of Tokyo to a four-year term. The TMG itself is divided into the **legislature** (the Tokyo Metropolitan Assembly, made up of 127 directly elected members) and **executive organizations** (comprising the governor and administrative commissions). Decision-making fundamentally resides with the Assembly, whose members, like the governor, serve for four years. The TMG administers city affairs jointly with the 23 *kuyakushō* (ward offices), each of which runs its own internal affairs and has its own mayor. The TMG runs citywide services such as the fire brigade.

Finance, Services and Industry

Tokyo has an estimated **800,000 businesses** and a daytime working population of over 8 million. Over 70 per cent of the workforce is now employed in tertiary industry, principally wholesaling, retailing, finance, real estate, transportation and services. Only around 20 per cent work in secondary industry, principally construction and manufacturing, which is carried out mainly along the coastal area between Tokyo and Yokohama, known as the **Keihin Industrial Region**. This region produces 20 per cent of Japan's manufactured goods, such as steel, chemicals, electronic equipment and optical goods.

The financial sector is concentrated around Marunouchi, Hibiya and Nihombashi. After a series of mergers, Japan's banks are now some of the largest in the world by assets, yet crippled by bad debts. The **Tokyo Stock Exchange**, once home to the second largest stock market in the world after the US, now functions largely as an administrative centre: all trading is conducted electronically. Under the impact of deflation, retailing has diversified significantly over the past decade away from the traditional department store towards a range of specialty stores such as Muji and Uniqlo, which now have an international presence.

THE PEOPLE
Ethnicity
The Japanese are fiercely proud of their ethnic homogeneity, yet are almost indisputably Korean in origin. The foreign population of Tokyo is over 250,000, of which the vast majority are Koreans, Chinese and Southeast Asians, followed by Brazilians, Americans and Europeans. Korean-Japanese relations still tend to be characterized by distrust, although Korean pop culture is now 'cool' to younger Japanese.

Education
Tokyo is not only one vast work and play machine; it takes education extremely seriously and has over 100 colleges and universities, not to mention thousands of kindergartens, regular schools and crammer schools, where anxious mothers send their children for extra tuition in the hope of getting them into one of the top institutions.

TOKYO LIVING

To be a resident of Tokyo means earning and producing more than people in the rest of Japan, while living in even more cramped conditions: nominal GDP per capita in the capital is ¥7.17 million (US$61,000) versus only ¥3.89 million (US$33,000) for the nation as a whole, while the average floor area of a home in central Tokyo is only 55m² (592 square feet), just two-thirds the national average. Commuters who work in Tokyo's central three wards travel an average of 70 minutes each way because they cannot afford housing close to their offices.

Religion

Two separate but inter-twining strands define the religious life of most Japanese. **Shinto (The Way of the Gods)** is an indigenous blend of animism and ancestor worship based around **kami**, spirits which reside in nature and souls of the departed. The emphasis of Shinto is life: fertility, marriage and other rites of passage. The major shrine in Tokyo is **Meiji Jingū** (*see* page 86). *Matsuri* (festivals) are a key element of Shinto: party-goers take to the streets and parade the kami around in a portable *mikoshi* (shrine).

Buddhism arrived in Japan from Korea in the 6th century and now thrives in the form of many different sects. Most Japanese are nominally Buddhist and have a Buddhist funeral. The oldest temple site in Tokyo is **Sensō-ji** at Asakusa (*see* page 50).

Christianity, which arrived with the Portuguese in 1549, has a lesser hold on Japan's religious life than numerous **new religious sects** such as the infamous **Aum Shinrikyō** (*see* page 34).

Language

Japanese has grammatical similarities to **Korean**. However, it is closer in some respects to the languages of **Austronesia** and the **Pacific Islands**, particularly in vocabulary and syllabic repetition (e.g. *peko-peko* = hungry, *guru-guru* = in circles).

Japanese is quite unlike Chinese. Chinese is monosyllabic, tonal and non-inflecting. Japanese is polysyllabic, non-tonal and inflecting. For an English speaker, pronouncing Japanese is no harder than pronouncing Italian. Syllables are **consonant-vowel combinations**

SUICIDE

Jisatsu (suicide) is seen as an acceptable way out of an impossible situation. In Japan the suicide rate has soared because of economic ills, overwork and school-bullying. Tokyo trains are virtually only ever delayed by people attempting suicide. Measures to brighten up the most popular 'suicide stations' have done little to deter the determined, but automatic barriers on newer subway lines such as the Namboku and Tōkyu Meguro extensions have proved more successful. *Seppuku* or *harakiri* (ritual suicide) refers to traditional disem-bowelment committed by a samurai wishing to follow his lord into death or to atone for shame. General Nogi (*see* page 90) and the novelist Mishima Yukio (*see* page 35) both committed *seppuku* out of imperial loyalty.

and are evenly stressed, e.g. *sake* (Japanese rice wine) = sa-ke. The place name Ikebukuro = i-ke-bu-ku-ro (not Aikabuckeroo). A macron sign denotes a long vowel, e.g. jū (ten) is pronounced as in 'joo'.

Loan words suffer from the fact that Japanese has no 'v' or 'l' sounds and often develop a different meaning e.g. '*Baikingu*' = Viking = buffet. Loan words are also often truncated, e.g. *wāpuro* = word processor.

Respect language is highly complex, requiring the altering of verb endings (or the use of different verbs altogether) to indicate **status**.

Writing

Japanese is written vertically from right to left and horizontally from left to right. Four systems are used together: *Kanji* (Chinese characters) form the backbone of the script; officially there are 1945 recognized *kanji* for items such as nouns and verbs. One *kanji* may have several sounds. Japanese also uses two phonemically identical but visually distinct syllabaries, **hiragana** and **katakana**, both originating in *kanji*. *Hiragana* is cursive and used to write grammatical elements. *Katakana* looks squarer and is used mainly for non-Chinese foreign words. Japanese also uses the **Roman alphabet** mostly for acronyms such as WTO.

Opposite: *Purification with incense is customary before visiting a temple.* **Left:** *This sign shows the* kanji *for Tokyo (the first two characters) and* katakana *for 'Joypolis'.*

Performing Arts

Tokyo offers a huge range of performing arts in a number of prime venues. Traditional drama is performed at
the National Theatre, the National Nō Theatre and the
Kabukiza in Ginza. *Nō* is a form of classical drama that
evolved in the 14th century. All actors are male and
speak in classical language virtually incomprehensible
even to native Japanese speakers. The *nō* stage is bare
apart from a pine tree backdrop; the action is slow and
elegant, revolving around the *shite* (principal character),
who wears a mask and fabulous brocade costume.

Kabuki is as showy and exuberant as the merchant
class of Edo Japan that patronized it (*see* page 64).
It too developed into an all-male theatre form in the
17th century, sustained by dynasties of actors famous
for sequences of prescribed movements ending in a *mie*
(climactic pose).

Mainstream classical concerts, ballet and international
musicals take place at Tokyo Opera City, NHK Hall,
Bunkamura and Suntory Hall. Contemporary stage arts
are shown at the New National Theatre in Shibuya.

Arts and Crafts

Japan is a paradise of traditional arts and crafts, ranging
from priceless objects to perfectly affordable items.
Ceramics include both rustic stoneware and porcelain;

Opposite: *The 'Flamme
D'Or' by Philippe Starck
is one of Tokyo's most
startling modern landmarks.*
Right: *Tokyo lacks garden
space, but potted plants
are used to brighten up
many balconies.*

lacquer is highly prized for its durability. Good presents include **bamboo baskets**, items of *washi* (Japanese paper), old textiles such as **second-hand wedding kimonos** and **obi** (belts), which can be used to good effect as wall hangings. *Tansu* (chests of drawers from the Edo and Meiji periods) make highly attractive, if expensive, pieces of furniture.

Architecture

The Japanese are lamentably unsentimental about their architectural heritage: much has been destroyed over the centuries either by catastrophe or in the spurious name of development. As a result, Tokyo has no distinguishing style as do London or New York. Instead, its grey vistas crisscrossed by a maze of telephone wires are occasionally alleviated by flashy **Western showpieces** from the 20th and 21st centuries. The only real continuity comes from temples and shrines, which are always rebuilt in traditional style.

The father of Western architecture in Japan was **Josiah Conder** (1852–1920), an Englishman, who in 1877 became professor of architecture at what is now Tokyo University. Conder's most famous work, dismantled in 1941, was the Rokumeikan, an elaborate Italianate building, where foreign dignitaries and the Meiji elite socialized and waltzed in Western dress. His remaining buildings include the Mitsui Club in Mita and the **Nikolai Cathedral** in Ochanomizu (*see* page 40). Neoclassical buildings by Conder's students visible today include the **Akasaka Geihinkan** (**Detached Palace**) completed in 1916, the **Bank of Japan** (1896) and **Tokyo Station** (1914).

THE IMPERIAL HOTEL

The Imperial Hotel exemplifies Tokyo's scrap and build attitude towards architecture. Opened in 1890, the first Imperial Hotel designed by Watanabe Yuzuru was a palatial neoclassical affair. Its second, highly exotic, incarnation designed by **Frank Lloyd Wright** (1867–1959) was a stone **Art Deco** construction reminiscent of a Mayan temple. Wright's creation opened just before the Great Kantō Earthquake of 1923, and not only survived the quake but was used as the disaster relief centre. In 1968, however, the marvelous construction was dismantled and its façade removed to Meiji Mura in Nagoya. The present Imperial Hotel gives little hint of its former architectural glory.

The Taishō Period (1912–26) saw the emergence of **Art Deco** influence exemplified by Frank Lloyd Wright's exotic **Imperial Hotel**, completed in 1922 (*see* page 23). Art Deco taste also lingered in early Shōwa-Period buildings such as the **Diet Building** completed in 1936 and the **Tokyo Metropolitan Teien Art Museum** (*see* page 76).

By 1945, however, vast swathes of Tokyo lay in ruins. Now, there was one priority: to fill the city's bomb-craters and to meet housing needs as quickly as possible. The result was cheap, eye-searing urban meltdown punctuated by new architectural symbols designed to instill hope for the future.

MOBILE PHONES

Compared with Taiwan's astonishing mobile phone penetration rate of 100 per cent, Japan has a long way to go, with only **65 million handsets** currently in use (one each for nearly 50 per cent of the population). Around 40 million handsets in Japan are Internet-enabled, which facilitates essential activities such as horoscope consultation by schoolgirls, who normally have two or three phones as fashion accessories.

Note that **foreign handsets do not work in Japan**. If you are staying in Japan for some time you can buy a cell phone with prepaid cards from NTT DoCoMo phone shops or electronics stores such as LAOX.

In 1960 a new movement called **Metabolism** was launched at the World Design Conference in Tokyo. Metabolism envisaged blending static infrastructure (freeways and parks) with dynamic modules (buildings) that could be changed as warranted by progress and technology. Key proponents include **Maki Fumihiko** (1928~) and **Kurokawa Kishō** (1934~), whose Nakagin Capsule Tower in Ginza (1972) is both dynamic and modular. The dynamism continues in ubiquitous cranes, which now form a permanent part of Tokyo's ever-evolving skyline.

Japan's most prominent architect since 1945 has been **Tange Kenzō** (1913~). His designs include **St Mary's Cathedral** (*see* page 105), completed in 1964; the **Olympic Stadium** (1964), the **Akasaka Prince Hotel** (1983), Shinjuku's **Tokyo Metropolitan Government Building** (*see* page 98), a soaring twin-tower office complex; and the **Fuji TV Building** (*see* page 71) in Tokyo Bay.

The stock market boom of the 1980s helped fuel ever bigger and more spectacular projects, turning Tokyo into a paradise for the world's leading architects.

Foreign-designed highlights include Philippe Starck's **Super Dry Hall** in Asakusa (1989) and Rafael Vinoly's **Tokyo International Forum** (*see* page 59), completed in 1996. The latest and biggest architectural showcase is **Roppongi Hills** (*see* page 93).

Sports and Recreation

The Japanese play harder now than ever before. To the vast majority of young women, shopping and TV soap operas are infinitely more important than traditional arts such as *ikebana* (flower arranging) or tea ceremonies. The average office worker is likely to prefer *pachinko* (*see* page 66), karaoke and *manga* (Japanese comic books or magazines) to martial arts such as Judo, Karate or Aikido.

Sumō and baseball are Japan's top two spectator sports, though soccer is rapidly catching up. *Sumō* is Shinto in origin, as all the accompanying paraphernalia and ceremony suggest. Pre-match posturing can take several minutes, but the bout itself lasts only a few seconds, ending in one of numerous classified 'throws'. Today's top *sumō* wrestlers are veritable human bulldozers weighing on average 156kg (343lbs), a hefty 30kgs (66lbs) more than in the 1970s. Becoming a *yokozuna* (grand champion) is a passport to instant national stardom.

Baseball became a professional sport in Japan in 1934 and has an obsessive following. The Central and

---

RELATIONS WITH KOREA

In 1910 Japan annexed Korea and subsequently imported many Koreans to work in Japan. Older-generation Japanese and Koreans still view each other with suspicion. Indeed, after the 1923 Tokyo earthquake, Japanese vigilante groups killed thousands of Koreans on suspicion of poisoning the city's wells. Nevertheless, Japanese-Korean relations have improved over the decades, as demonstrated by the once unthinkable idea of both countries co-hosting the **World Cup** in 2002. Younger generation Japanese have now developed an insatiable taste for **Korean pop culture** and food, which despite its spiciness is now ultra 'cool'.

Opposite: *A new mobile phone is a Japanese girl's best friend.*
Left: *Baseball is one of the top spectator sports in Japan.*

Pacific Leagues each have six teams. **Soccer** too has caught on in a big way since the establishment of the J-League in 1993. Its standing has only been enhanced by Japan's and South Korea's co-hosting of the World Cup in 2000.

Tokyo boasts about 500 **golf driving ranges**, where businessmen can practise their swing within the safety of green nets before venturing out for a highly expensive round on one of the capital region's 90 or so golf courses.

Food and Drink

Tokyo has a massive range of international cuisine, but to make the most of any visit to Japan you need an adventurous approach.

Japanese cuisine comes in numerous different forms. At the top end of the range is *kaiseki-ryōri*, the Rolls Royce of traditional food, which originated in the 16th century as a simple accompaniment to the tea ceremony but developed into endless, exquisitely prepared tiny dishes of fish, vegetables, meat and rice accompanied by *sake* or beer. *Kaiseki* is served by kimono-clad waitresses in highly elegant surroundings, often in a room with a garden view. It is a cultural, aesthetic and highly expensive experience.

Below: Sembei *(rice crackers) make a great snack on the run.*

At the other end of the range comes *shōjin-ryōri*, Zen Buddhist cuisine based on *tōfu* and *sansai* (mountain greens). This delicious array of vegetarian cuisine served as a set meal is available at special restaurants in both Tokyo and Kamakura, but is not necessarily cheap.

Tōfu (soybean curd) comes in numerous forms ranging from *hiya-yakko* (blocks of *tōfu* served cold

with soy sauce, ginger and bonito shavings) to *agedashi-dōfu* (deep-fried *tōfu* served with grated *daikon*, or radish).

Nabe (stew) is another staple dish usually cooked at the table over a gas burner. Ingredients range from seafood and meat to leeks, cabbage, *tōfu* and *shiitake* (mushrooms). Noodles may be added at the end. *Chanko nabe* is a high-protein mélange of fish, meat and vegetables that fuels *sumō* wrestlers.

Above: Sake *comes in a variety of bottles, or flagons (*tokkuri*).*

The ubiquitous ***bentō*** (lunch box) ranges from beautifully prepared lacquer trays of rice and vegetables to the take-away ***eki-ben*** (station lunch box), an often unspeakably disgusting fusion of cold rice and congealed tempura.

Other sticky items – deliberately so – are ***kashi*** (Japanese cakes) which accompany green tea: *Yōkan* is bean jelly and *mochi* is a glutinous rice dumpling.

Drinking is a national pastime. Each year the Japanese quaff millions of kilolitres of **beer** and **sake**. Japanese lagers such as Asahi, Kirin and Sapporo are the most popular brews, although Guinness has also arrived big time.

Sake is made from fermented rice and comes in a variety of grades (like whisky) and brews as familiar to *sake* connoisseurs as different grape varieties are to oenophiles. However, *sake* does not improve with age and is usually drunk during the year of manufacture. *Sake* can be served hot (*atsukan*) or cold and is always delicious when drunk out of a *masu* (small square wooden box). ***Nama-zake*** (raw *sake*) is unpasteurized *sake* strong enough to easily put you under the table.

Shōchū, distilled from rice, barley or potatoes, is like rough vodka, but can be good. Whisky is the drink of bars. Wine consumption is growing rapidly; some progress has been made in growing Chardonnay and

---

SOME POPULAR DISHES

donburi – hot rice with different toppings
oden – stew with fish cake
okonomiyaki – DIY Japanese pancake
rāmen – Chinese-style noodles
sashimi – slices of raw fish
shabushabu – thin beef dipped in sesame sauce
soba – thin buckwheat noodles
sukiyaki – thin beef dipped in sweet sauce
sushi – fish on vinegared rice
tempura – battered prawns and vegetables
tonkatsu – deep-fried pork
yakitori – grilled skewers of chicken
udon – fat white noodles
unagi – grilled eel

Cabernet Sauvignon grapes in Japan, but France and Australia need not worry about their wine exports yet.

Shopping

Tokyo is one gigantic shopping mall, where everything is available all the time. Prices began to come down in the 1990s and there are now thousands of convenience stores, discount stores and even ¥100 stores. Even so, visitors in their right mind do not go to Japan to buy a *Gucci* handbag.

Department stores are cradle-to-grave institutions encompassing art galleries, restaurants, food halls, designer gear, wedding and even funeral services. **Mitsukoshi** in Nihombashi and **Isetan** in Shinjuku (which has a Foreign Customer Service Centre) are two worthy examples of the genre.

For the extraordinary spectacle of a Virtual Italy in Japan, go to **VenusFort** (*see* page 73). For prime boutique locations, try **Daikanyama** (*see* page 81) and **Shimokitazawa** (*see* page 103).

Akihabara (*see* page 41) is Tokyo's **consumer electronics** capital, where all kinds of products-from the first colour TVs to the first DVD players have made their consumer debut since World War II. Stores also carry export models. **West Shinjuku** (*see* page 98) is famous for **cameras**. **Kanda** (*see* page 38) is the home of second-hand **bookshops** and **skiwear**. **Kappabashi** (*see* page 51) is the place for kitchen equipment and the plastic food models that appear in many restaurant windows

There are still many traditional arts and crafts shops in Ginza, Nihombashi and Asakusa. The **Japan Traditional Craft Centre** in Aoyama (*see* page 91) has a whole range of items, but **flea markets** (*see* side panel) provide the best fun for picking up ceramics and old kimonos.

FLEA MARKETS

One of Tokyo's pleasures is rooting around at antique and flea markets for ceramics, old kimonos and bric-a-brac. Atypically for Japan, you are expected to bargain. The best buys go early; activity winds down through the afternoon. Fairs may be cancelled in the event of rain. Some popular venues include:
Nogi Shrine (Nogizaka): second Sunday of the month.
Tomioka Hachiman-gū (Ryōgoku): On the first of the month, and second Sunday.
Tōgō Shrine (Harajuku): first and fourth Sundays.
Hanazono Shrine (Shinjuku): every Sunday.
Roppongi Antique Fair (ROI Building): fourth Thursday and Friday of the month.
Yasukuni Shrine: third Sunday of the month.

Nightlife

From the most exclusive **Ginza** club to the **Irish pub**, via the *Nō-pan Kissaten* (No Panty Coffee Shop), where the waitresses wear little more than an apron, Tokyo night life is one long adult version of Alice in Wonderland. Drink is what lubricates the wheels of business in Japan – never mind pleasure – and money will buy anything: the spirit of Yoshiwara is alive and well.

The most respected businessman will be forgiven anything when drunk, but no one is forgiven for failing to pay the bill. Many bars and clubs will not accept credit cards and have a hefty cover charge. The damage to both health and wealth can be immense, so find out what you are paying for before you start.

The traditional hangout for *gaijin* (foreigners) has been **Roppongi** (*see* page 92) ever since the Americans adopted it during the Occupation. Crammed with expensive bars, restaurants and clubs, it throbs all night.

In **Ginza** and **Akasaka** politicians arrive in fleets of black limousines for a discreet evening's entertainment by a *geisha*, while the young, mobile-phone brigade hangs out in **Shibuya** (*see* page 82). At the end of a long night **Shinjuku** (*see* page 98) wins hands down for sleaze: **Kabukichō** (*see* page 100) is the heart of all things naughty from live sex shows to Pink Cabaret; **Shinjuku Ni-chome** is the heart of **Gay Tokyo**, where *gaijin* must tread carefully to gain acceptance (*see* panel, page 101).

KARAOKE

To the Japanese, karaoke (lit. 'empty orchestra') is an art form. There are even books and magazines on '*The Way of Karaoke*'. Unsuspecting foreigners cornered in a bar may cringe at the idea of being expected to belt out a Beatles song to a taped soundtrack. But the Japanese take a dim view if you refuse to perform. Drinking copious amounts of *sake* will help get over the embarrassment. Karaoke has grown into a massive industry since its humble origins in the 1970s; it is also one of the few forms of Japanese popular culture to have caught on in the West.

Opposite: *Shopping arcades like this offer everything from clothes to coffee shops.*
Left: *The Sanai Building at Yon-chome crossing is an integral part of Ginza's neon night-scene.*

2
Around the
Imperial Palace

For all its apparently chaotic change and random growth over the centuries, the city of Tokyo still radiates out in concentric circles from the Imperial Palace at its heart. The main difference between now and the 17th century is that present-day **Imperial Tokyo** takes up only a fraction of the area once occupied by the Edo Castle of the Tokugawa *shōguns*. This chapter takes you on a clockwise tour from south to north inside **Sotobori-dōri** (Outer Moat Road), now semi-encircled by subway lines. For areas east of the palace (including Hibiya) *see* Chapter 4.

Highlights of the palace area include the remaining moats and walls, particularly Nijū-bashi, Chidorigafuchi Moat (popular for its cherry blossoms in spring) and the palace garden of Higashi Gyoen. Much as in the Edo Period (1600–1868), when the residences of feudal lords surrounded the old castle, the wheels of **Political Tokyo** now turn from Kasumigaseki and Nagatachō, home to the National Diet Building. Nearby highlights include the **Suntory Museum of Art** and Hie Shrine.

The **Yasukuni Shrine** and War Memorial Museum to the north provide highly disturbing reminders of World War II, but there is a lighter atmosphere further east along Yasukuni-dōri, where **Intellectual Tokyo** hangs out in the mildly bohemian bookshops and cafés of **Jimbōchō**. From the Nikolai Cathedral of Ochanomizu to the Kanda Myōjin Shrine and the mind-boggling maze of electronics shops in **Akihabara**, this northeast corner of Central Tokyo is fun to explore.

DON'T MISS

*** **Imperial Palace Gardens:** moats and cherry trees.
*** **Suntory Museum of Art:** exquisite decorative arts.
** **Kanda Myojin Shrine:** venue of the spectacular Kanda festival.
** **Yasukuni Shrine and War Museum:** monuments to Japan's war-dead.
** **Jimbōchō bookshops:** the heart of intellectual Tokyo.
** **Akihabara:** Tokyo's neon electrical goods Mecca.

Opposite: *Rowers admire cherry blossoms overhanging Chidorigafuchi Moat.*

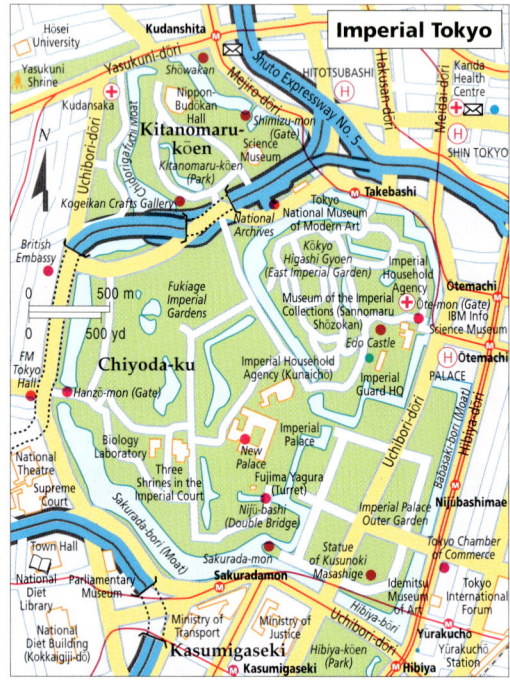

IMPERIAL TOKYO

Modern imperial Tokyo is so unobtrusive as to be virtually comatose: you will not get to see Crown Princess Masako popping out like the late Diana Princess of Wales for a spot of shopping. But in a city short of greenery, the palace area is perfect for a stroll into history through the soaring outer walls of Edo Castle that still flank the palace moat.

Imperial Palace Gardens **

When Tokugawa Ieyasu, made Edo his headquarters in 1590, he began constructing his castle on the site of the first fortification built by Ōta Dōkan in 1457. By 1640, **Edo Castle** was the largest fortification in the world with 19 keeps, 30 bridges and 100 gates. Today, the Imperial Palace is but a shadow of the old castle's glory: bombed in World War II, it was largely rebuilt in 1968.

The inner grounds of the Palace beyond **Nijū-bashi** are open only on 2 January and the Emperor's birthday (23 December). However, the view of Nijū-bashi and the **Fujimi Yagura** (one of only three original 17th-century keeps) near the Sakurada-mon is freely available to everyone and is one of the most photographed spots in Tokyo. Close to the palace is the Kunaichō (Imperial Household Agency), the institution that preserves arcane imperial tradition and ceremonies.

Two areas are open to the public. On the northern edge of the main palace grounds, **Chidorigafuchi Moat** is one of Tokyo's top cherry blossom-viewing spots – if you can tolerate the crowds shuffling beneath the blossoms and queuing for rowing boats. Meanwhile, a stroll through **Higashi Gyoen** (**East Imperial Garden**) still gives some idea of the scale of Edo Castle: Bairinzaka (Plum Slope), which leads up to the site of the original donjon burned down in 1657, takes its name from plum trees that were first planted by Ōta Dōkan. The **Sannomaru Shōzokan** (Museum of the Imperial Collections) by the Ōte-mon displays some of the Emperor Shōwa's items donated to the government in 1989. Both Higashi Gyoen and the Sannomaru Shōzokan are open 09:00–16:00 Tuesday–Thursday, Saturday–Sunday (until 15:30 November–February). Admission free. (To enter the gardens take a token at the gate and return it on departure.)

Kitanomaru-kōen, the northernmost park, is home to the **Nippon Budōkan**, a striking octagonal-shaped martial arts hall built for the 1964 Olympics, and the **Science Museum**, which is popular with children for its interactive exhibits. Open 09:30–16:30 daily. For more information visit the website: www.jsf.or.jp

Kogeikan
(Crafts Gallery) **

The Crafts Gallery is an annex of the nearby **National Museum of Modern Art**. Housed in an attractive 1910 Meiji-Period brick building, the gallery is a good place to familiarize yourself with Japanese crafts such as ceramics and textiles. Open 10:00–17:00, Tuesday–Sunday. The National Museum of Modern Art itself has recently undergone a facelift and offers world-class exhibits.

IMPERIAL SUCCESSION

Tradition has it that the imperial family is descended from the sun goddess Amaterasu. Even so, since 1868 only male heirs have been allowed to inherit the Chrysanthemum Throne. On 1 December 2001 **Crown Princess Masako**, the Harvard-educated, multi-lingual wife of **Crown Prince Naruhito**, gave birth to **Princess Toshi**, the couple's first child. Given that no male has been born into the imperial family since 1965, there is now talk of extending the laws of succession to female heirs.

Below: *Cherry blossom-viewing is one of Japan's long-established rituals.*

Below: *The mighty
parabolic walls and moat
of the present Imperial
Palace once protected the
shōguns in Edo Castle.*

POLITICAL TOKYO

Japan is effectively governed from Kasumigaseki and
Nagatachō. Kasumigaseki is home to **government
bureaucracies** ranging from the Ministry of Finance to
the Ministry of Foreign Affairs. The finest building is the
Ministry of Justice (1895), which survived the 1923
earthquake, but was damaged in 1945. Nagatachō,
immediately to the west, is the heart of **Political Tokyo**,
where the Prime Minister has his Official Residence and
where Diet members congregate before heading in black
limousines to the bars and clubs of Akasaka and Ginza
to conclude the private deals that drive Japanese politics.

The National Diet Building (**Kokkaigiji-dō**) is a pon-
derous Art Deco structure completed in 1936. The House
of Representatives (the Lower House) meets in the South
Wing and the House of Councillors (Upper House)
meets in the North Wing. Tours of the Diet Building are
normally conducted in Japanese only and subject to sus-
pension if the Diet is in session.

For serious researchers of Japan, the **National Diet
Library** is open 09:30–17:00 Monday–Friday (except
Mondays following the 1st and 3rd Saturdays of the
month, public holidays and refiling days). The library
has an excellent website at www.ndl.go.jp/en

Nearby, facing the inner moat, is the **Supreme
Court**, followed by the **National Theatre**, which stages
traditional Japanese performing arts such as *nō* and
bunraku (*see* page 22).

Hie Shrine *

West of Nagatachō, just behind
the Capitol Tōkyu Hotel, is the
Hie Shrine (also known as Sannō
Shrine) first established by Ōta
Dōkan in 1457 to guard his castle.
Marked by a sparkling blue sign
and lanterns, this quiet hilltop
offers a moment's peaceful con-
templation between business
appointments. Beyond, the dome

of the Diet Building is just visible. In even-numbered years, from 10–16 June, the Shrine hosts the Sannō Matsuri, one of Tokyo's three great festivals, which alternates with the Kanda Matsuri, held in odd-numbered years (*see* page 40). The festival features ox-drawn carriages in a costumed procession.

Suntory Museum of Art ***

Opposite the New Ōtani Hotel in the Suntory Building is one of Tokyo's top fine-arts museums. The Suntory Collection of 3000 Japanese art items ranging from paintings and ceramics to textiles and stunning glassware is one of the very best in Tokyo. A small portion of works is displayed at any one time in imaginative exhibitions accompanied by English explanations. '**Beauty in the midst of life**' is the museum's guiding principle. Open 10:00–17:00 Tuesday–Sunday, until 19:00 on Fridays. Tokyo Suntory Building, 11th Floor, Moto Akasaka 1–2–3, Minato-ku. Closest station: Akasaka Mitsuke, Marunouchi line. For full details see www.suntory.co.jp/sma

North to Yasukuni Shrine

Though a rather anomalous area today, Kōjimachi, north of the National Theatre, was the great diplomatic district of the Meiji Period. The grandest remaining architecture here belongs to the **British Embassy**, which has stubbornly stuck to its exclusive enclave in Ichibanchō on the inner moat, even though other major embassies are now

Right: *The Hie Shrine near the Capitol Tōkyu Hotel is one of Tokyo's oldest, dating from the mid-15th century.*

located elsewhere. By far the most elaborate architecture of all, just outside Sotobori-dōri, is the **Akasaka Detached Palace (Geihinkan)**. Completed in 1908, this neoclassical extravaganza of Versailles-meets-Buckingham-Palace by Katayama Tokuma (a student of Josiah Conder) is now used exclusively for visiting heads of states and diplomats. It is open to the public via a draw of names on only 10 days each year. Tours are conducted in Japanese.

Yasukuni Shrine and Yūshūkan
(War Memorial Museum) **

A grim steel *torii* (shrine gate) marks the beginning of the long cherry tree-lined avenue leading to the Yasukuni Shrine. Established in 1869 by the Emperor Meiji, Yasukuni (Peaceful Country) enshrines the souls of Japan's war dead. According to Yasukuni's official website, the Shrine is dedicated to **2,466,000** *kami* (spirits), not only from World War II, but from all conflicts since the fall of the Tokugawa *shōgunate*.

When Emperor Hirohito renounced his divinity on 1 January 1946, the links between Shinto (*see* page 20) and nationalism were officially cut. Yet, each year controversy rages at home and in the rest of Asia when the prime minister or members of his cabinet arrive at the Shrine on 15 August to commemorate Japan's war dead: is this an act of official or personal homage?

Yasukuni is home to **1000 cherry trees**. When the blossoms emerge in early April, the grounds take on a party atmosphere as people picnic and buy food from *yatai* (stalls) beneath white doves circling above. It is hard not to view the cherry blossoms as symbolic of the World War II kamikaze pilots whose brief lives are also commemorated here.

The austere **Yūshūkan** (War Memorial Museum) adjacent to the Shrine is Tokyo's most disturbing sightseeing spot. Despite a recent facelift, the museum is still inhabited by ghosts, which dominate a present that has consistently failed to confront its past. Outside sits the C5631, the first locomotive to pass the junction at the opening of the infamous **Thai-Burma Railway**: the Japanese labelling briefly 'prays for the repose of those

---

KAMIKAZE

Kamikaze (divine wind) refers to a typhoon that repelled the Mongols during their attempted invasion of Kyūshū in 1281. In 1944 the term was hijacked by the Japanese military to denote a new unit of Air Force **suicide attackers** chosen to strike Allied warships and regain momentum behind the Pacific War. Suicide attacks destroyed at least 40 American ships in the Pacific and 16 in the Philippines; the **Battle of Okinawa** saw over 2000 missions. Volunteers were teenage idealists trained to avoid 'wasting' experienced pilots on one-off missions. All swore allegiance to the emperor and hoped to avoid the ignominy of returning alive.

Below: *Prizes at a Yasukuni Shrine fair demonstrate Japan's love of cuddly toys.*

KOISHIKAWA KŌRAKU-EN

Just north of Sotobori-dōri by The Tokyo Dome (aka Big Egg) and Kōraku-en Amusement Park is Tokyo's oldest and most famous **Edo-Period garden** dating from 1629. Now only a fraction of its original size, it is still a pleasant place to escape into an extraordinary world of rice paddies, irises and vistas that recreates famous Chinese and Japanese natural scenes such as Arashiyama in Kyoto. The only drawback is the hideous urban landscape beyond, particularly the parachute tower of the amusement park. Open 09:00–17:00, daily. Closest station: Iidabashi, Namboku line.

MISHIMA YUKIO (1925–72)

Mishima Yukio achieved international renown both for his literary output (including 20 novels such as *The Temple of the Golden Pavilion*) and for his dramatic death. Homosexual, yet married, Mishima adulated the traditional values of the **samurai**, even leading his own militaristic group, the Tate no Kai (Shield Society). On 25 November 1972 Mishima took General Mashita hostage inside the headquarters of the Jieitai (Self-Defence Force) before addressing members of the Jieitai from a balcony: when they rejected his appeal for a return to traditional samurai values, he returned inside to commit ritual suicide.

who lost their lives constructing the railway'. Inside, exhibits include cannons, human torpedoes, an imperial fighter plane, gloves, spectacles, poems and poignant final diary entries of **kamikaze pilots**, whose youthful faces stare out from black and white photographs. Open 09:00–16:30 daily, until 16:00 November–Februrary.

Diagonally opposite Yasukuni Shrine on Yasukuni-dōri, is the titanium-fronted **Shōwakan**, Tokyo's latest offering to the memory of the late Emperor Hirohito. It presents an anodyne and much criticized portrayal of World War II. Open 10:00–17:30, Tuesday–Sunday. No English labelling. A visit for diehards only.

INTELLECTUAL TOKYO

The **Kanda** area northeast of Imperial Tokyo is extensive, encompassing educational establishments such as Nihon University, Meiji University and the Tokyo Dental College. Though the analogy is far-fetched, Kanda's **Jimbōchō** district along Yasukuni-dōri is Tokyo's version of the Left Bank in Paris. Jimbōchō is still very firmly 'high city', where **Intellectual Tokyo** browses in secondhand bookstores and reads over coffee – even if that mostly means Starbucks these days.

Kanda also takes a liberal approach to religion, boasting the Russian Orthodox **Nikolai Cathedral** near Ochanomizu station, the **Yushima Seidō** (a Confucian shrine) and the Shinto shrine of **Kanda Myōjin**, not to mention **Akihabara**, the Mecca of Electronics. The most striking modern landmark along the dingy-looking Kanda River parallel to Sotobori-dōri, is Norman Foster's **Century Tower**, headquarters of the Nomura Research Institute.

Jimbōchō **

The Rolls-Royce of Jimbōchō's bookstores is **Kitazawa Shoten** on Yasukuni-dōri. Kitazawa Shoten was established in 1902 and stocks over 40,000 new books (1st floor) and 30,000 imported antiquarian books (2nd floor). It is well worth taking a look behind this elegant granite-clad exterior solely to marvel at the arcane foreign titles on offer, which range from Beowulf to Kierkegaard.

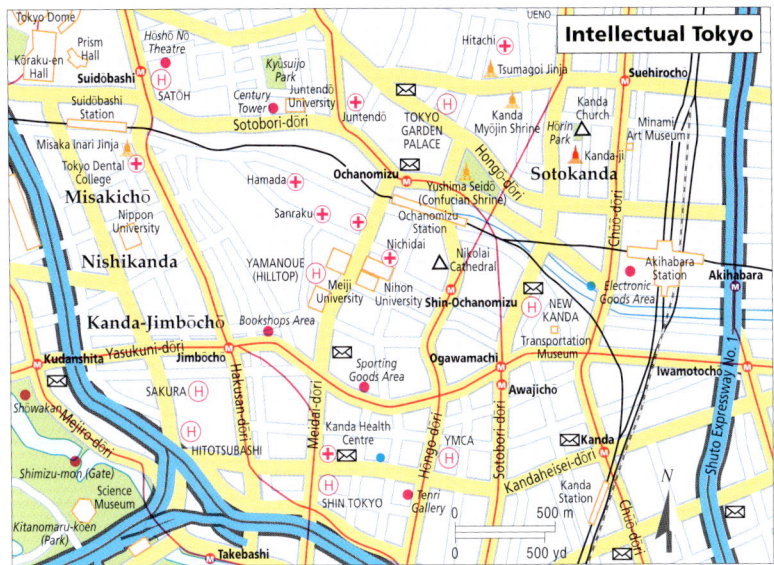

Take virtually any turning off Yasukuni-dōri around here and you will enter a more prosaic world of businessmen browsing old *manga* along back streets lined with rusting balconies and higgledy-piggledy façades that give the faintest hint of Taishō Japan in the 1920s. There are plenty of cafés and restaurants to while away the time.

East along Yasukuni-dōri is a jungle of sporting equipment shops, which sell the latest ski and snow-boarding wear. Along Meidai-dōri (north of Yasukuni-dōri) towards Ochanomizu is **Meiji University**, which offers a couple of quirky museums in the Daigaku Kaikan Building on Meidai-dōri itself: the **Criminology Museum** on the 4th floor is heavily into methods of torture used in the Edo Period (1600–1868) and has little English labelling; the **Archaeological Museum** on the 3rd floor has good English labelling and some excellent Yayoi Period (300BC–AD300) pottery. Both museums are open 10:00–16:30 Monday–Friday, till 12:30 on Saturday. Admission free.

CONFUCIAN VALUES

The study of the **Chinese sage**, **Confucius**, gained momentum in Japan in the 17th century as the Tokugawa *shōguns* realized that the Confucian value of **loyalty** between ruler and subject, father and son and husband and wife provided highly suitable underpinning for their feudal order. The effects linger within Japanese social structure, which hinges on a series of asymmetrical relationships, now increasingly strained by the breakdown of the extended family and lack of job security. Confucius also advocated **compromise**, not conflict, which may explain the Japanese tendency to avoid litigation.

Opposite: Akihabara is one of the largest electrical equipment retailing centres in the world.

Just beyond, left up Surugadai Hill (virtually opposite Ochanomizu Square), is the old-fashioned **Yamanoue (Hilltop) Hotel**, (*see* At a Glance, page 117). Since it first opened in 1954, the 'Hilltop' has been a favourite place with writers, including Mishima Yukio.

Nikolai Cathedral •

The street by Ochanomizu station is a musicians' Akihabara, with numerous shops selling a huge range of guitars. Along Hongō-dōri towards Shin-Ochanomizu station is the Tokyo Holy Resurrection Church, known popularly as the **Nikolai-dō** (Nikolai Cathedral), after the Russian priest, Nikolai, who arrived in Tokyo from Hakodate in 1872. This striking onion-domed creation – Japan's largest Byzantine construction – was built under the supervision of Josiah Conder from 1884–91. Anyone may attend services on Saturday evenings or Sunday mornings or visit between 13:00–15.30 Tuesday–Friday. However, these official hours can be hit and miss, so be prepared to return if necessary.

Just beyond Sotobori-dōri is the less exotic **Yushima Seidō**, a Confucian Hall which burned down four times during the Edo Period (1600–1868) and did not survive the Great Kantō Earthquake of 1923. The present ferro-concrete edifice is best visited on weekends, when the hall is open. The Niitoku Gate, however, dates from 1704 and is an Important Cultural Treasure. Down the steps to the right, in a shady spot, is a monumental statue of **Confucius** himself.

Kanda Myōjin Shrine ••

The present Kanda Myōjin Shrine, which is dedicated to a 10th century rebel called Taira no Masakado, is a concrete replica of a 17th-century building destroyed in the 1923 earthquake. The charming lion fountain in the courtyard, however, is thought to date from the Edo Period. This shrine is also the focus of the **Kanda Matsuri** held in mid-May in odd-numbered years. It develops into a riotous parade of *mikoshi* (portable shrines) through the streets of Kanda, Ōtemachi and Nihombashi.

TOKYO'S THREE BIG FESTIVALS

Tokyo's three big festivals all take place in summer:
The **Kanda Matsuri** in mid-May starts at the Kanda Myōjin Shrine and features 70 *mikoshi* (portable shrines), which wend their way on the last day through Kanda, Ōtemachi and Nihombashi. The festival is held in odd-numbered years.
The **Sanja Matsuri**, on the third weekend of May, is held at the Asakusa Shrine (see page 51). This was the great *shitamachi* (low city) festival in Edo days and still attracts huge crowds.
The **Sannō Matsuri** at the Hie Shrine is held in mid-June in even-numbered years. Ox-drawn carriages and mounted samurai make their way around the palace to Ginza and Kyōbashi.

Akihabara **

Popularly known as **Electric Town**, though its literal translation is Field of Autumn Leaves, Akihabara was originally the site of the Akiba Shrine, whose grounds were cleared as a firebreak in Edo times. After World War I, Akihabara became a bicycle wholesaling district, but its origins as Tokyo's neon-lit Mecca of **electrical goods** lie in the radio, the nation's key information medium at the time of the emperor's surrender broadcast in 1945. After 1945, stalls selling spare parts for radios sprang up around the station, where the Sōbu and Yamanote lines intersect. Subsequently, every cutting-edge electronic item made its debut in Akihabara, from the first colour TV to the slimmest cellular phones and notebook computers. Today the area is one mind-boggling rabbit warren of thousands of shops packed into a narrow grid-work of streets reminiscent of Bangkok or Hong Kong.

For the first timer, the least confusing option is to go to one of the big stores such as LAOX, Yamagiwa, Nishikawa or Daiichi Katei Denki, which normally have helpful English-speaking staff and offer export models **Duty Free**.

Transportation Museum *

Akihabara also became an important transport centre in the Meiji Period, so it is appropriate that the area is home to the Transportation Museum, which is immediately recognizable by the *shinkansen* (bullet train) sticking out of its front wall. From the first steam locomotive to run between Shimbashi and Yokohama in 1872 to a model of a magnetically levitated train, the museum is a fun place to view a variety of road, maritime and air transport. Open from 09:30–17:00 Tuesday–Sunday.

THE JAPANESE TOILET

Nowhere does the Japanese obsession with gadgets and bodily functions converge more neatly than the toilet, which in Japan is a designer item. Toilets at stations are usually of the primitive squatting variety: take your own supply of free tissues (*see* page 67). However, toilets at department stores and even in the average home often have control panels fit for the flight deck of a Boeing 747: heated seats, tunes to mask the sound of urination; jet-spray bidet functions and a blow-dry are all integral to that most personal of experiences.

3
Old Tokyo

Old Tokyo is not a picture postcard given that the *shitamachi* (low city) areas of Asakusa, Ryōgoku and Fukagawa bore the brunt of both the 1923 earthquake and the air raids of 1945. Nevertheless these areas also afford a welcome glimpse of the past and flashes of an earthy resilience against the otherwise relentless internationalization of Tokyo.

Ueno is virtually a city in itself, encompassing one of Tokyo's major railway stations, its first public park and several cultural venues including the world-class **Tokyo National Museum**. Much more off the beaten track is nearby **Yanaka**, where you can wander along back streets dotted with temples and some small museums.

Yanaka is actually more evocative of a bygone era than **Asakusa**, the official face of Old Tokyo. Asakusa is now a shadow of its once boisterous past, yet remains a top attraction on account of the **Asakusa Kannon Temple** and the small shops of Nakamise-dōri, not to mention Philippe Starck's startling 'Golden Flame' sculpture, which dominates the riverside where boats arrive from Hinode Pier.

East of the river is Ryōgoku, home to the **National** *Sumō* **Stadium**, *sumō* stables, *chanko nabe* restaurants and the impressive **Edo-Tokyo Museum**. *Sumō* fans should also not miss the Yokozuna Monument of the Tomioka Hachiman Shrine. Other worthwhile diversions include the **Kiyosumi Teien**, a garden oasis in the urban jungle, and the **Tokyo Museum of Contemporary Art**, which has a world-class international collection.

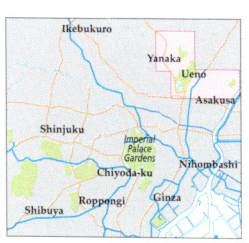

DON'T MISS

*** Tokyo National Museum: stunning 7th-century Hōryū-ji treasures.
*** Yanaka: temples, a cemetery and small museums.
*** Asakusa Kannon Temple (Sensō-ji): Tokyo's oldest temple site.
*** Edo-Tokyo Museum: high-tech history museum.
** Kappabashi Kitchenware Town: from plastic food to chopsticks.
** Fukagawa Edo Museum: an intimate look at the past.
** Kiyosumi Teien: a pleasant Edo-Period garden.

Opposite: *Asakusa Kannon Temple was founded in AD628.*

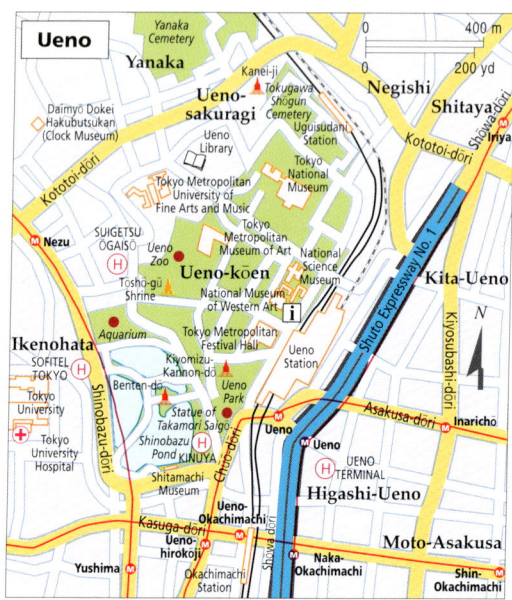

UENO

Ueno is a curious hodge-podge of both order and chaos, slightly flaky at the edges with pretensions to grandeur. To the west it is flanked by prestigious Tokyo University, yet to the south it retains the rough edge of *shitamachi* ethos, particularly in its bars, *rakugo* (comic monologue) theatres, as well as 'soaplands' (a euphemism for brothels). UenoPark is a popular cherry-blossom viewing venue and home to the world-class **Tokyo National Museum**.

Ueno Park **

In 1868 Tokugawa loyalists made their last stand against forces loyal to the Emperor Meiji at Ueno. **Kanei-ji**, the guardian temple of the Tokugawa clan which extended over a vast area north and east of Shinobazu Pond, was severely damaged. After 1868, the government decided to use the area for a new medical school. However, **Dr Baudin**, a Dutchman, suggested turning it into a park, which it duly became in 1873. Ever since, the crowds have come flocking.

The only 17th-century buildings now within the park are the **Tōshō-gū** (a somewhat dilapidated but charming shrine dedicated to Ieyasu, the first Tokugawa *shōgun*) and the five-storey pagoda, which actually stands within Ueno Zoo (the latter is far from one of Tokyo's top attractions). A smaller-scale Kanei-ji is now located behind the Tokyo National Museum towards Uguisudani JR station, adjacent to an overgrown cemetery where six of the 15 Tokugawa *shōguns* are buried.

CARDBOARD CITY

Over the past decade **Ueno Park** has become home to a growing number of homeless Japanese brought low by recession. At cherry blossom time, when more than two million people come to party under a canopy of delicate pink petals, for the briefest of periods the gap between the down-and-outs and the fully employed is bridged by a common choice of exterior decor: blue tarpaulins to sit on and cardboard boxes to act as tables and shelter. Both social classes dutifully remove their shoes before sitting down on their tarpaulins: living rough and picnicking still require exacting standards.

The southern half of the park is best explored from Ueno station's Shinobazu exit. On the right is a statue of **Takamori Saigō**, a leading imperial loyalist in 1868 whose forces opposed the Tokugawa *shōgunate*. Diagonally opposite is the Kiyomizu Kannon-dō, a miniature – and infinitely paler – version of the famous Kiyomizu Temple in Kyoto that stands on stilts.

Beyond is **Shinobazu Pond**, a charmingly weedy spot, where lotus blossoms flower in summer and wildfowl take refuge from the ever-encroaching concrete. The small shrine projecting into the water is dedicated

AMEYOKO-CHŌ

Ameyoko-chō (Candy Sellers' Alley), which runs parallel with the tracks from the Shinobazu exit of the JR station towards Okachimachi station, provides a back-to-basics shopping experience reminiscent of London street markets. Ameyoko-chō began as a **black market** after World War II: here, cheap sports shoes and bags vie for space with fresh fish, dried squid and the Japanese sweets from which the market gets its name (although 'Ame' may also derive from 'American', harking back to the days of the Occupation when American goods were on sale). Ueno also has a handful of **traditional shops** such as Jūsanya, which has made combs for 250 years.

Left: *General MacArthur wanted this statue of Takamori Saigō removed after 1945 because of its nationalistic overtones. It survived.*

HŌRYŪ-JI TREASURES

Hōryū-ji, southwest of Nara, is Japan's most remarkable Buddhist temple site, both for its age and quality of architecture and objects dating from the 7th century. In 1878 the Imperial Household donated over 300 of Hōryū-ji's treasures to the **Tokyo National Museum**, where the **Hōryū-ji Hōmotsukan** at the National Museum has six galleries displaying 7th- and 8th-century gilt-bronze statues, paintings, calligraphy, textiles, mask and lacquerware. Although nothing substitutes for a visit to Hōryū-ji itself (which boasts the world's oldest wooden building), the National Museum exhibits are both stunning and unique.

Below: *The Tokyo National Museum, established in 1871, is Japan's most important collection.*

to Benten, the Goddess of Fortune. Over 100 years ago, the Emperor Meiji came here to watch horse racing on a track around the pond.

MUSEUMS

Ueno's major museums (with the exception of Shitamachi Museum by Shinobazu Pond) are in the north of the park. The **Tokyo Metropolitan Museum of Art** stages modern Japanese works of art. Open 09:00–17:00, daily, except the third Monday of each month. The **National Science Museum** deals with subjects from astronomy to natural history, but is less interactively oriented than the Science Museum in Kitanomaru Kōen. Open 09:00–16:30 Tuesday–Sunday.

Tokyo National Museum ***

Until the addition of two new wings in 1999, the Tokyo National Museum got full marks for content, but low scores on presentation. Now, Japan's top art collection is infinitely more digestible. The jewel in the crown is the new **Hōryū-ji Hōmotsukan** (Gallery of Hōryū-ji Treasures). If you have limited time, make this gallery alone your priority.

Of the other buildings, the **Honkan** (main building) houses the permanent collection of Japanese Arts; the

Tōyōkan displays Asian Art and antiquities and the neoclassical **Hyōkeikan** has occasional special exhibitions. The new **Heiseikan** has a permanent Japanese Archaeological Gallery on the first floor and special exhibitions on the second floor. Open 09:30–17:00, Tuesday–Sunday (until 20:00 on Fridays, April–December). For information on galleries and exhibitions, see www.tnm.go.jp

National Museum of Western Art **

This museum houses pre-18th century art in the main building, designed by the French architect Le Corbusier (1887–1965), and 19th and 20th century works in the New Wing. The museum also has 58 sculptures by Auguste Rodin. Open 09:30–17:00, Tuesday–Sunday, and until 20:00 on Fridays. Entry is free on the second and fourth Saturdays of the month. See www.nmwa.go.jp for details of major exhibitions.

Above: *Rodin's* The Burghers of Calais *stands outside the National Museum of Western Art.*

Shitamachi Museum *

This is the most intimate and old-fashioned of Tokyo's three museums devoted to Old Tokyo. It has examples of shops, houses, a rickshaw and a wide variety of objects ranging from hats, kitchen utensils and pocket watches to black-and-white photographs of the way life used to be. Open 09:30–16:30 Tuesday–Sunday.

YANAKA

Yanaka, just north of Ueno, survived both the 1923 earthquake and the 1945 bombings largely intact. Though only 20 minutes by Chiyoda line from the rush of central Tokyo, Yanaka is a secluded world, where writers and artists have created a virtual extension of Kanda. Here, carefully tended pot plants brighten the urban jungle and cats sun themselves as you stroll along back streets dotted with temples, galleries and traditional craft shops.

From Nippori station (Yamanote line), a walk up the hillside takes you into **Yanaka Reien**, one of Tokyo's first public cemeteries, created in 1874. Fresh flowers and incense adorn a few of the 6000 graves, which include those of literary figures and the last Tokugawa *shōgun*. The rest look rather more forlorn.

SCAI THE BATHHOUSE

In the days when few citizens of *shitamachi* had their own washing facilities, the **sentō** (bathhouse) was a place to chat as well as to bathe. Tokyo's public bathhouses have dwindled over the decades (or turned into more dubious venues). **Scai the Bathhouse**, a converted bathhouse with 7m (23ft) ceilings and spectacular natural light conditions, has become one of Tokyo's showcases for young contemporary artists. Open 12:00–19:00 Tuesday–Sunday. Scai is on Kototoi-dōri, 6-1-23 Yanaka, Taito-ku. Closest station: Nezu, Chiyoda line.

Above: *The quiet back streets of Yanaka provide respite from the bustle of the city centre.*

Yanaka Temple Town owes its origins to the plethora of sub-temples of Kanei-ji established in the 17th century, as well as to temples moved here after the Great Fire of 1657. The best known is **Tennō-ji** (close to Nippori station) whose pagoda was destroyed in 1957 by arson. The area situated between Shinobazu-dōri, Kototoi-dōri and Sansakizaka contains both many temples and a worthwhile couple of museums and galleries. On Kototoi-dōri is the **Shitamachi Museum Annex**, a restored *sake* storehouse. Open 09:30–16:30, Tuesday–Sunday. Admission free.

Asakura Sculpture Museum (Chōsō Museum) ✶✶

Near the cemetery, the Asakura Sculpture Museum is an idiosyncratic shrine to the works of Asakura Fumio (1883–1964), one of Japan's early 20th-century sculptors. Though heavy on bronze busts, Asakura's work also has a playful note, as demonstrated by his sculptures of cats. The exhibits suffer from a lack of English labelling, but the building and tranquil Japanese garden are both charming. Open 09:30–16:30, Tuesday–Thursday and Saturday–Sunday. Closest station: Nippori, Yamanote line.

Daimyō Dokei Hakubutsukan (Daimyō Clock Museum) ✶✶

This dark, dusty, one-room collection of clocks made for the *daimyō* (feudal lords) of Tokugawa Japan was established by Kamiguchi 'Guro', proprietor of an early 20th-century Western-style clothing store. Ask for a copy of the excellent leaflet in English on the history of *daimyō* clocks and the telling of time in Japan. Open 10:00–16:00

YAYOI PERIOD (300BC–AD300)

The Yayoi Period (300BC–AD300), when migrants from the Korean peninsula brought paddy rice farming and crop cultivation to Japan via Kyūshū, takes its name from the Yayoi district in Bunkyō-ku, now home to Tokyo University. Finds in the late 19th century of pottery sherds at a site next to Yayoi called Mukōgaoka revealed new styles of pottery that denoted a clear break with the preceding Jōmon Period (10,000–300BC).

Tuesday–Sunday, 16 January – 30 June and 1 October – 24 December. (Ring the doorbell if the museum appears to be shut during official opening hours.) Closest station: Nezu, Chiyoda line.

Nezu Shrine **

Just northwest of Nezu station and Shinobazu-dōri is the atmospheric Nezu Shrine, where it is still just about possible to imagine samurai striding along in sumptuous costume. The buildings, many of which date from the early 18th century, are best viewed in early spring when a breathtaking array of azaleas come into bloom. Nezu also has an attractive avenue of small *torii* (shrine gate) leading to an *inari* (fox) shrine.

ASAKUSA

Asakusa was the heart of *shitamachi* during the Edo Period, where merchants could watch *kabuki* (*see* page 22), drink tea and generally relax.

By the 1920s, it had become a thriving theatre, cinema and cabaret district, dominated by the newly built Ryōunkaku, an audacious 12-storey skyscraper 67m (220ft) high, which, along with most of Asakusa, collapsed during the 1923 earthquake.

Now, the skyline is dominated by Philippe Starck's 'Golden Flame' sculpture, which marks Asahi Brewery's headquarters by the river. The sculpture's nickname of 'the turd' is in keeping with Asakusa's tradition for earthiness, which has never been diminished by its alter ego as a pilgrimage site.

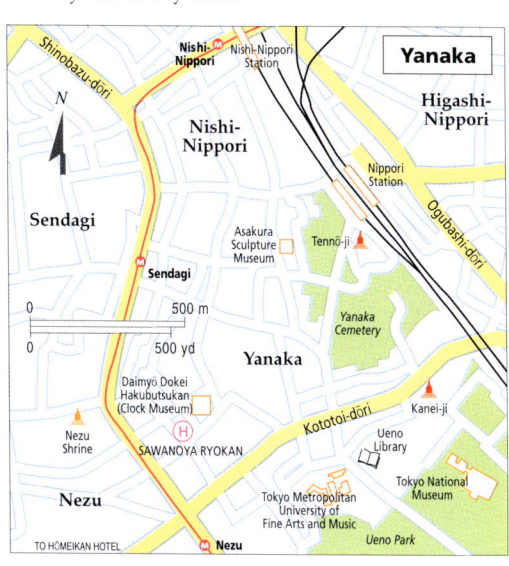

ASAKUSA FESTIVALS

Golden Dragon Dance: 18 March and 18 October.
Sanja Matsuri: third weekend in May. Tokyo's biggest festival focused on the Asakusa Shrine. A riotous procession of *mikoshi* (portable shrines).
Sumida River Fireworks: late July to early August.
Brazilian Samba Festival: Late August.
Tokyo Jidai Matsuri: 3 November. Re-enactment of historical scenes.
Hagoita-ichi (Batteldore Fair): December. Stalls sell elaborately decorated battledores. Check with the Asakusa Information Centre opposite the Kaminari-mon for full details.

When the **Hanayashiki Amusement Park** first opened in 1853 it had caged animals on display. Even now it is very old-fashioned compared with the high-tech of Disneyland, but the roller coaster and ghost house are still popular attractions. Open 10:00–18:00, closed Tuesdays.

Beyond is the Rokku district, the seedier end of cinemas and porn shows, and home to the Engei Hall, where the actor 'Beat' Takeshi appeared early in his career.

Sensō-ji (Asakusa Kannon Temple) ★★★

Asakusa's impressive **Kaminari-mon** (Thunder Gate) is immediately recognizable by its enormous red lantern; it is also guarded on either side by the gods of wind and rain, posing like two *kabuki* actors. Beyond lies **Nakamise-dōri**, an alleyway packed with shops selling *sembei* (rice crackers), toys, dolls, traditional combs, umbrellas and paper wallets. There is a festive atmosphere here all year round, but Asakusa also has more than its fair share of Tokyo's festivals.

In front of the two-storey treasure gate, is the **main hall** of **Asakusa Kannon**, as the temple is popularly known. According to tradition it was founded in AD628 to house a tiny gold statue of **Kannon** (the goddess of mercy) caught in the nets of two fishermen. The present

Right: *Sensō-ji (Asakusa Kannon Temple) is the official heart of Old Tokyo and a popular place on weekends.*

building dates only from 1958, though it is hard to tell. In front, high-heeled teenagers and wizened elderly people stop at an imposing bronze censer to purify themselves by wafting plumes of incense over their heads.

The other landmarks include the 17th-century **Asakusa Jinja** (Shrine) on the right, dedicated to the two Kannon fishermen, and on the left, the reconstructed **pagoda**, which belongs to the **Dembō-in** (Abbot's Residence). The garden is not normally open to the public.

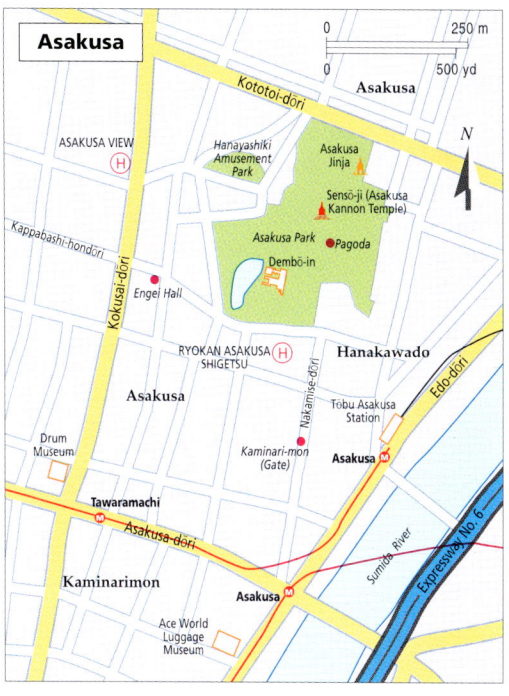

Kappabashi – Kitchenware Town **

In Japanese, *kappa* means both 'raincoat' and 'water sprite'. Although the original bridge of Kappabashi was destroyed in 1933, legend has it that the name derives from a raincoat seller, who obtained the help of a water sprite living in the Sumida River to build a local waterway.

Whatever the truth of the story, you cannot miss Kappabashi at the corner of Asakusa-dōri heading towards Ueno: Tokyo's kitchenware district is marked on one side by an enormous head with a chef's hat on top of the Nimi Building and on the other by a building whose corner consists of gigantic stacked plastic cups and saucers.

Along the main street, and in several side streets, around **200 shops** sell fearsome knives, forks, rice cookers, bowls, chopsticks, signboards and waiters' uniforms to the catering and restaurant industry.

Kappabashi is a good place to pick up reasonably priced Japanese **plates** and **bowls** for everyday use. You can also buy from Maizuru and Tokyo Biken (on the main street) plastic models of food that restaurants use to display their menus: realistically moulded French bread, cheese, fruit and sushi may sound distinctly low-tech, but these inedible works of art cost much more than their edible counterparts.

There is another unusual shopping area on Akasaka-dōri, where a row of stores sells attractive family **Buddhist altars** ranging from opulent heavy wooden and gold-leaf models to sleeker varieties more suitable to the modern home.

RYŌGOKU

East of the Sumida River, Ryōgoku was flattened in the 1923 Great Kantō Earthquake. Around 40,000 people died in the ensuing fires in the area now known as the **Jishin Kinen Kōen** (Earthquake Memorial Park), recognizable by its pagoda and museum (open 09:30–16:00 Tuesday–Sunday, admission free). The park also commemorates those who died in the bombings of 1945.

CHOPSTICK ETIQUETTE

There is just as much etiquette attached to eating prettily with chopsticks as to eating with a knife and fork. Try and keep the lower chopstick (which rests between the base of the thumb and the index finger) perfectly still, while controlling the movement of the upper chopstick with the top joint of the index finger so that the tip of the upper chopstick moves up and down to meet the tip of the lower one. When not eating, place the tips of your chopsticks on the small ceramic *hashi-oki* (chopstick rest) by your place setting. Do not spear or scoop up food, or point with your chopsticks.

Nearby are the gardens of Kyū Yasuda Teien, a small Edo-Period garden where admission is also free.

Ryōgoku's biggest claim to fame is the **National Sumō Stadium** (Kokugikan), describable from the station by its green roof. Tournament tickets are expensive; a cheaper option is to visit a *sumō beya* (*sumō* stable) to watch an early morning practice session. (Ask your hotel to phone in Japanese.) At the very least you are likely to see wrestlers shuffling along the streets like elephantine cherubs. (Note that only the top-ranked wrestlers wear top-knots.) Ryōgoku is also the place to try *chanko nabe*, the high-protein stew that fuels *sumō* wrestlers.

Edo-Tokyo Museum **

In the opposite direction, but close to Ryōgoku station is the **Edo-Tokyo Museum**, which uses a high-tech environment to trace Tokyo's 400-year evolution from feudal castle town to cosmopolitan capital. The museum exterior is an eyesore, but the interior is well labelled in English, with life-size replicas and audiovisual displays on topics ranging from samurai life to the bombing of Tokyo. For exhibition information see www.edo-tokyo-museum.or.jp One ticket is valid for re-entry all day. Open 09:30–17:30 Tuesday–Sunday, until 20:00 Thursday–Friday.

SUMŌ INFORMATION

Japan has six annual *Sumō* tournaments, each lasting two weeks from the Sunday closest to the 10th of the month. Tokyo hosts the January, May and September tournaments (*bashō*) at **Kokugikan**, the National *Sumō* Stadium. The March tournament is held in Ōsaka; July in Nagoya and November in Fukuoka. Check out the official *Sumō* Association website: www.sumo.or.jp for ticket information, tournament schedules and real-time match updates. During Tokyo tournaments, the small **Sumō Museum** next to the National Stadium by Ryōgoku station is open only to spectators. At other times it is open 10:00–16:30. Admission free. Be sure to pick up the highly informative English leaflet on *sumō*.

Opposite: *Point and order: plastic food displays make it easier to choose when eating out.*
Left: Sumō *wrestlers hold onto each other's* mawashi *(belt) as they grapple in the* dohyō *(ring).*

Opposite: *Not quite the*
canals of Amsterdam, but
a cruise on the Sumida
River has its own merits.

SOUTH OF RYŌGOKU

Down Kiyosumi-dōri, the main road leading south from
the Edo-Tokyo Museum, Fukugawa has several other
attractions in this area once inhabited by the merchants
of *shitamachi.*

Fukagawa Edo Museum **

Less chaotic than Ueno's Shitamachi Museum – and
much less high-tech than the Edo-Tokyo Museum – the
Fukagawa Edo Museum is the most digestible of Tokyo's
three museums dedicated to life in Edo. Here one can
wander the streets of a replica 19th-century riverside district complete with canal,
shops and warehouses.
Open 09:30–17:00 daily.
Closest station: Kiyosumi-
Shirakawa, Ōedo line.

Kiyosumi Teien (Garden) **

This small Edo-Period
garden is best enjoyed by
ignoring the ugliness of the
skyline beyond. In the
Meiji Period the estate
belonged to the Iwasaki
family, who in 1909 built
the elegant Ryōtei teahouse
for a visit by Field Marshal
Kitchener of Khartoum.
Today gulls and ducks
enjoy this green oasis as
much as Tokyo's hassled
citizens. The views are
particularly pretty in May
and June when the irises
and azaleas are in bloom.
Open 09:00–17:00 daily.
Closest station: Kiyosumi-
Shirakawa, Ōedo line.

Museum of Contemporary Art, Tokyo ★★

The Museum of Contemporary Art in Kiba Park is a breath of fresh air: built in an amalgam of architectural styles, it offers cavernous galleries, an art library, an art information centre and a good cafeteria, though its funding is presently in jeopardy. Exhibitions from the permanent collection of 3000 Japanese and international post-World War II art are rotated six times a year. For information on temporary exhibitions see www.mot-art-museum.jp Open 10:00–18:00 Tuesday–Sunday. Closest station: Kiba station, Tōzai line.

Tomioka Hachiman Shrine ★

Sumō fans should not miss the huge Yokozuna Monument behind this shrine. It records the names of all *sumō* wrestlers who have gained top champion (*yokozuna*) status in the sport's history. A full version of the spectacular Fukagawa Festival is held here in mid-August every three years (the next is due in 2005).

TOKYO CRUISES

One of the best ways to see Old Tokyo is to take a 40-minute cruise up the Sumida River from Hinode Pier (near Hamamatsuchō station) to the water-bus station by Azuma Bridge in Asakusa. The boat passes under 12 bridges and passes sights such as Tsukiji Fish Market, Tsukudajima and the National *Sumō* Stadium. **Tokyo Cruise Ship Co.** runs cruises at regular intervals in both directions. Other routes from Hinode Pier include a harbour cruise under Rainbow Bridge; a canal cruise to Shinagawa Aquarium, and Kasai Sealife Park in Tokyo Bay via Palette Town and Tokyo Big Sight. www.suijobus.com

4
From Marunouchi to Ginza

The eastern edge of the Imperial Palace is flanked by **Establishment Tokyo**, where banks, company headquarters and venerable department stores all have a long-established presence. This chapter divides Marunouchi, Yurakuchō and Hibiya (the areas west of Tokyo station's omnipresent railtracks) from Nihombashi, Kyōbashi and Ginza, which lie to the east, outside Sotobori-dōri. On the west side, be sure to visit Rafael Vinoly's **Tokyo International Forum** and the **Idemitsu Museum of Art**.

On the east side, Nihombashi is both the heart of *shitamachi* Edo and also the focus of **Financial Tokyo**. The area is rather staid and stodgy, and you are unlikely to spend much time here unless you are on business, though the **Bank of Japan** is worth a look.

Ginza has grown up since the 1920s, when *Gin-bura* (strolling the Ginza) was as cool an activity as hanging out in Shibuya is now. These days shops such as Wakō, Mikimoto Pearls, Kyūkyodō and Tiffany's give Ginza the air of a stately dowager duchess, though the grid system of minor roads behind offers a less formal wealth of smaller shops, art galleries and elite bars. The **Sony Building** is a must for technophiles.

In Higashi (East) Ginza, the **Kabuki-za** offers a theatrical glimpse of old Edo en route to **Tsukiji Fish Market**, the world's most intense seafood experience. If you can ignore the urban jungle beyond, the gardens of **Hama Rikyū-en**, at the mouth of the Sumida River, are also well worth visiting.

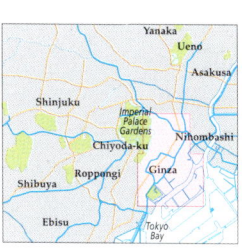

DON'T MISS

*** Tsukiji Fish Market: tuna capital of the world.
** Tokyo International Forum: eye-catching architecture.
** Idemitsu Museum of Art: a premier Oriental art collection.
** Sony Building: a chance for technophiles to play.
** Hama Rikyū-en: a haven in the urban jungle.
** Kabuki-za: the flamboyant home of kabuki theatre.

Opposite: *Ginza has come a long way from gaslight and the horse-drawn trolley.*

Marunouchi ('within the moat walls') is where the most trusted feudal lords built their residences during the Edo Period. Once feudal power disintegrated and the lords went home to the provinces, this huge area of land adjacent to the palace became vacant. The 'meadow', as it was known, was taken over by the **Mitsubishi** family in 1890 and began its transformation into the business district, flanked by Ōtemachi to the north, which today houses banks and media headquarters, and Yūrakuchō and Hibiya to the south. Marunouchi feels relatively spacious, in keeping with the adjacent palace grounds.

Tokyo Station, which is modelled on Amsterdam station, opened in 1914. It survived the 1923 earthquake largely intact and its façade today offers a serene glimpse of Meiji-Period brick architecture that masks beneath and behind a rabbit warren of shopping malls, tracks and concourses stretching through to the Yaesu side. Each day, over 4000 JR trains pass along the 25 platforms of Tokyo station, which employs 800 station staff. If you have time to kill, visit the **Tokyo Station Gallery** (Marunouchi side), which exhibits a variety of art displays. Open 10:00–19:00 Tuesday–Friday, till 18:00 on weekends.

The latest landmark is the newly rebuilt **Marunouchi Building**, which now rises 180m (591ft) above the business district and offers an attractive range of shops and

Opposite: *TIF, Tokyo International Forum, is one of the capital's architectural statements.*

restaurants with good views from the top floors of the Imperial Palace, Akasaka, Roppongi and beyond.

Yūrakuchō, the next station south on the Yamanote line, is convenient for institutions such as the Imperial Hotel (*see* page 23), the new Takarazuka Theatre (famous for its musicals staged entirely by women), cinemas, restaurants and, should you need tickets for DisneyLand, the Tokyo Disney Resort Ticket Centre Office (*see* page 72). In an alleyway rumbling with vibrations from the overhead railway tracks, reminiscent of Liza Minelli's scene beneath the arches in *Cabaret*, Yūrakuchō also offers *yatai* (food stalls), where you can point-and-order snacks such as *yakitori*.

Nearby **Hibiya Park** was once a military parade ground, as its bandstand testifies. Though a poor relative of New York's Central Park in scale, Hibiya is pleasant enough on spring days when office workers take lunchtime strolls among the rose bushes.

Tokyo International Forum (TIF) ⁕⁕

The daring, parabolic glass- and steel-built TIF is one of Tokyo's pieces of flagship architecture. Designed by Rafael Vinoly, the TIF was opened in 1996 and hosts conferences, exhibitions and concerts, as well as shops and restaurants. The two main theatres, Halls A and C, seat over 5000 and 1500 people respectively, but so cavernous is the superstructure that it easily accommodates such huge numbers.

Idemitsu Museum of Art ⁕⁕

Although the Idemitsu Collection is one of the world's greatest Oriental art collections, its tiny Tokyo space does it little justice. Exhibitions range from ceramics to Buddhist paintings and rotate frequently. Open 10:00–17:00,

SPECIAL EVENTS

Apart from Tokyo's Big Three Festivals, here are a few others to note:
6 January: Dezome-shiki parade by Tokyo's fire brigades, who perform stunts on ladders along Chūo-dōri in Harumi.
3 February: Setsubun bean throwing at temples such as Zōjō-ji and Asakusa.
Sunday closest to 17 March: St Patrick's Day Parade, Omotesandō.
Early August: Takigi (Torchlit) Nō at Hie Shrine.
3 November: Meiji Jingū Autumn Festival with yabusame (mounted archery).
14–15 December: Gishi-sai costumed festival at Sengaku-ji commemorating the 47 *rōnin* (see page 74).

Below: *All action at the Tokyo Stock Exchange is electronic these days.*

Tuesday–Sunday. Teikoku Geki-jō Building, 9th Floor, 3-1-1 Marunouchi, Chiyoda-ku. Closest station: Yūrakuchō, Yamanote line.

FINANCIAL TOKYO

The Yaesu exit of Tokyo station disgorges thousands of workers into offices and corporate headquarters along Chūō-dōri, which stretches from **Nihombashi** in the north to **Ginza** in the south. Though dreary, Nihombashi still hints at flashier times, as demonstrated by the Art Deco-style entrance of **Mitsukoshi**, Tokyo's most venerable department store, which has occupied the same spot by the bridge of Nihombashi since 1673. As the doyenne of its genre, Mitsukoshi is a cradle-to-grave institution, offering everything from wedding to funeral gifts, as well as a veritable banquet of foods on its basement floors, and Chanel and Louis Vuitton on the ground floor.

Picturesque images of the actual bridge of Nihombashi, where the major highways of the Edo Period converged, now figure only in old wood-block prints such as Hiroshige's *Fifty-Three Views of the Tōkaidō*. The present bridge is rather more prosaic, sitting glumly beneath a tortuous network of highways. In a continuation of tradition with Edo days, however, the wrought-iron pillar next to the bridge still marks the centre of the city. To get a feel for the original bridge you need to walk across the replica in the **Edo-Tokyo Museum** (*see* page 53).

The **Bank of Japan** (BOJ), close to Mitsukoshi, is the only Meiji-Period building still standing in Nihombashi. Sited on the spot where the Ginza silver mint moved to in the 19th century, it was designed by one of Josiah Condor's Japanese pupils,

Tatsuno Kingo (1854–1919). Construction was completed in 1896.

You can only penetrate this fortress of monetary inscrutability by calling ahead to join a group tour. Open from 10:00–15:00 Monday–Friday; tel: (03) 3729 1111. Admission to the Currency Museum opposite the BOJ is free. Open from 09:30–16:30 Tuesday–Sunday.

For a slight diversion en route to the **Tokyo Stock Exchange** (TSE) in Kabutochō, try the **Kite Museum** on the fifth floor above Taimeiken, an old Western-style restaurant. The museum houses a chaotic floor-to-ceiling jumble of 2000 kites from all around the world. Open from 11:00–17:00, Monday–Saturday.

Visiting the TSE is a rather hollow experience now that computers have

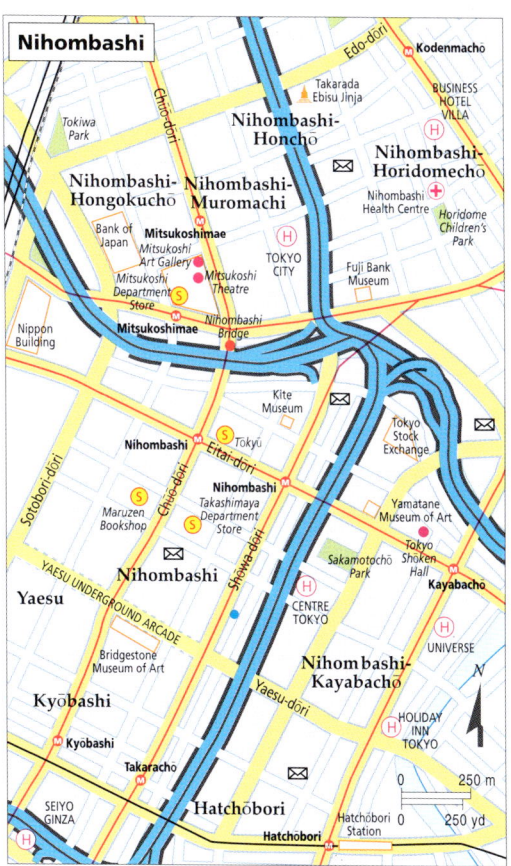

eliminated the trading floor once reminiscent of Wall Street. All that remains is a cylindrical glass structure, where administrative functions are carried out. The **TSE Historical Museum** gives a perspective on the past. Visiting hours are 09:00–16:00 Monday–Friday.

Back on Chūō-dōri, opposite Takashimaya Department Store, is **Maruzen**, which has been selling books on this spot since 1870. Maruzen has a good foreign-language section, though English language books are not cheap in Japan. Towards Ginza, at the corner of

Ukiyo-e

Ukiyo-e (woodblock prints) became popular in the 18th century, covering a huge range of subjects from courtesans, *sumō* wrestlers and *kabuki* actors to flowers, birds and landscapes. Meiji-Period prints began to depict urban subjects such as railways.

Chūō and Yaesu-dōri is the **Bridge-stone Museum of Art**, one of Tokyo's premier Western art museums. Open 10:00–20:00 Tuesday–Friday, until 18:00 on weekends.

GINZA

Ginza means 'silver seat' owing to the fact that during the Edo Period the *shōguns* minted their silver coinage here. Like Shimbashi, Ginza was also a major *geisha* centre, as well as home to the Komparu troupe of Nō Theatre actors, whose name lingers on in the old Komaparu Yū bathhouse in Komparu-dōri, behind Shiseido and parallel with Sotobori-dōri.

Ginza's rise to elegance was initially fanned by the **Great Fire of 1872**, which resulted in a new town of red brick buildings and willow-lined boulevards that fulfilled the desire for all things Western. The gaslight made its debut in 1874, and the horse-drawn trolley in 1883. Until the brick collapsed in the Great Earthquake of 1923, *Gin-bura* (strolling the Ginza) was a popular past time, as was hanging out in smart cafés.

Gin-bura is back, particularly on Sundays, when Chūō-dōri is open to pedestrians only. Le Café Doutor Espresso, Japan's smartest Doutor Coffee Shop, at the corner of Ginza Yon-chōme (perhaps Tokyo's best known crossroads), is one of the cheaper places to people-watch. The surrounding buildings include the elegant **Wakō** department store, dating from 1932, a new Nissan Gallery and, next to Le Doutor, **Kyūkyodo**, a traditional paper shop selling incense, writing brushes and *washi* (handmade paper). Other venerable institutions include Mitsukoshi and Mikimoto Pearls, which has a pearl museum. Despite the 1990s collapse in property prices, Kyūkyodo is still reportedly Tokyo's most expensive patch of real estate per square metre.

DEPARTMENT STORE ROOFTOPS

Rather like New Delhi, Tokyo takes on a new perspective above ground level; whereas the inhabitants of Delhi like to race pigeons from their rooftops, the Japanese keep carp-filled ponds and pet departments on high. **Mitsukoshi** and **Takashi-maya** in Nihombashi also have Chelsea Garden shops, where Tokyoites buy their spring plants and dream of their very own English gardens. On top of Mitsukoshi, Ginza Yon-chome, is a shrine to Shusse Jizō, the guardian deity of Ginza. This small statue was unearthed during the Meiji Period and placed on the roof in 1968 for long life and prosperity.

Sony Building **

The Sony Building, at Sukiyabashi crossing, is every technophile's dream, offering the opportunity to play with a range of Sony's latest toys, from the most sophisticated laptop computer to the most exciting computer game. The chromium, futuristic environment makes a simple statement: here is the cutting edge of consumer electronics technology. There are restaurants and cafés on every floor, including, at the premium end, Sabatini's (Italian), Maxim's (French) and Ginza Tenichi (a high-quality tempura restaurant).

Higashi Ginza and Tsukiji

Heading towards Higashi (East) Ginza, the architecture starts to lose its monolithic quality, degenerating into a more chaotic mixture of old wooden buildings and drab, anonymous blocks occasionally punctuated by the more original creation. The most conspicuous edifice is the elaborate wedding cake-style facade of the **Kabuki-za** on Harumi-dōri.

Down the road to the right of the Kabuki-za, the newly opened **Ki no Hana** coffee shop caught the eye of John Lennon and Yoko Ono on 4 August 1979. The famous couple left behind a cartoon that adorns the wall, thereby assuring the owner eternal fame in a land that still worships The Beatles.

Back in the early 1860s, however, foreigners were far from worshipped: indeed, initially they were kept at bay in a settlement not far from the present Tsukiji Fish Market. Among the legacies of this era are Rikkyō (St Paul's) University and St Luke's Hospital, which still occupies its original site.

Opposite: *A quiet moment flower-shopping in the back streets of Ginza.*
Below: *Wakō department store – one of Ginza's most august institutions.*

Kabuki-za **

The new Kabuki-za theatre marked the transition of the merchant class's favourite entertainment from the low to the high city when it opened in 1889: respectability had arrived. The present building dates from 1925.

Kabuki still has a devoted following in Japan; queues for tickets start early in the day and a full performance lasts several hours. English earphone guides are essential to help follow the plot, even though the impact is over-whelmingly visual. Tickets to watch one act only (earphones not available) are sold on the day. The box office is open from 10:00–18:00.

Tsukiji Hongan-ji *

Further down Harumi-dōri en route to Tsukiji Fish Market is the extraordinary Gothic-Indian façade of **Hongan-ji** rebuilt in 1935 after the 1923 earthquake. The cavernous interior of this bizarre building has both a golden altar draped in brocades and immense chande-liers; here the homeless take a quiet snooze at the back, while businessmen drop in on their way to work. On 24 January 1971, Hongan-ji hosted Mishima Yukio's memo-rial ceremony, a suitably gaudy venue for one of Japan's most flamboyant authors (*see* panel, page 38).

Right: *Billboards outside the Kabuki-za fail to draw a younger Japanese audience.*

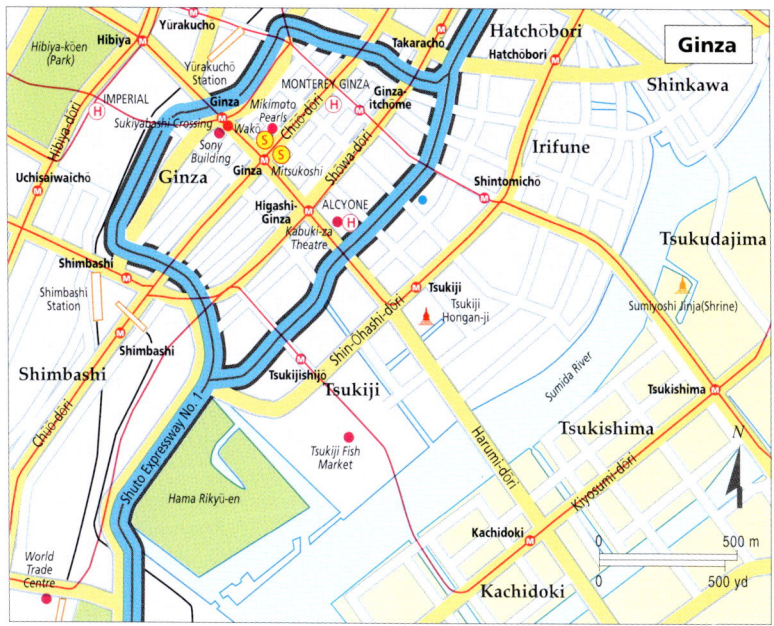

Tsukiji Fish Market ***
(The Tokyo Metropolitan Central Wholesale Market)

Tokyo's first fish market was established in Nihombashi over 400 years ago. These days the action takes place at Tsukiji, where the tuna auction at the world's biggest fish market gets underway around 05:30. Visitors are not officially allowed to attend the auction, but wholesalers generally ignore spectators who hang around at the back. Watching your back is essential – once buyers start removing their catch of frosted tuna torpedoes, a rush of forklift trucks manned by manic drivers means taking your life in your hands. Do not cross open spaces or aisles without first looking both ways. Also do not wear your best shoes: the floor is slippery and fish merchants wear gumboots for a good reason.

After the auction, fearsome mechanical saws are used to reduce whole tuna carcasses into more manageable pieces for restaurateurs to take away down aisles

> **FISHY FACTS**
>
> The Japanese are one of the world's largest fish consumers, gobbling around 70kg (155lb) per person annually. Here are some names to remember when eating *sushi* or *sashimi*:
> *amaebi* – sweet prawn (raw)
> *hamachi* – yellow tail
> *ebi* – prawn (boiled)
> *ika* – squid
> *ikura* – salmon roe
> *maguro* – tuna
> *tai* – sea bream
> *tako* – octopus
> *toro* – fatty tuna
> *uni* – sea urchin

Above: *Make an early start if you want to catch the action at Tsukiji.*

crammed with baskets of dusky pink octopus, giant clams, live eels and fat, juicy prawns.

For a fresh **sushi** breakfast try one of the cramped restaurants in the grey barrack-type buildings in front of the market. The market is closed on Sundays and public holidays. Also note that Tokyo authorities are apparently planning to move the market to a nearby site within a couple of years.

Tsukudajima *

A short walk across the Sumida River from Tsukiji is Tsukudajima, which was first inhabited by fishermen from western Japan in the 1600s, who came at the invitation of Tokugawa Ieyasu to supply the rapidly growing settlement of **Edo** with fish. The fishermen also probably acted as spies for the *shōgun* on the traffic plying his waterways.

For now, this quiet enclave of old houses and fishing boats, marked by the Ishikawajima Lighthouse and Sumiyoshi Shrine, stubbornly resists the onslaught of new high-rise developments. Somehow, the ghost of Edo lingers on in the cry of the gulls. For a view from the water, take a Sumida River cruise up to Asakusa from Hinode Pier or Hama Rikyū-en (*see* panel, page 55).

AROUND SHIMBASHI

In the Meiji Period, **Shimbashi** ('New Bridge') was the grand terminus for the first railway between Tokyo and Yokohama, which opened in 1872. It was also a prime *geisha* quarter, but assumed a less prominent position after Tokyo station opened in 1914. In 1995, however, Shimbashi took on a new role as gateway to the futuristic city being built on reclaimed land out in Tokyo Bay, by becoming the terminus for the unmanned Yurikamome

---

PACHINKO

Pachinko is a cross between playing pinball and slot machines. It is one of Japan's national pastimes, as you will see from the gaudy parlours evident all over Tokyo, where grandmothers, businessmen and students sit compulsively ogling balls that shoot up inside the machine and then settle in slots, which spins windows of pictures or numbers. Matching windows produce a reward in the form of more balls, which you can go and exchange first for prizes, then for money – around ¥2.5 per ball. Mindless though *pachinko* may appear, professionals can make big bucks.

monorail. Shimbashi itself has little real attraction, although it is a fairly popular after-hours drinking destination for office workers.

At Hamamatsuchō, the next stop south on the Yamanote line, is another much older monorail, which makes the 20-minute journey to Haneda Airport. From the top of the ageing **World Trade Centre** there is a reasonably good view of Rainbow Bridge and the Bay area, though with so many free city views now available, there is little compelling reason to pay the admission fee. Directly by Hamamatsuchō station is a small Edo-Period garden called Kyū Shiba Rikyū-en, a smaller version of Hama Rikyū-en.

Hama Rikyū-en **

One charming spot by the water is Hama Rikyū-en, which was originally an estate owned by the Matsudaira family before it became the duck-hunting grounds of the Tokugawa *shōguns* in the mid-17th century. Bridges and islets dot this graceful garden, which also has a tidal pond. The skyline beyond is invariably lined with the cranes that persistently accompany Tokyo's ever-changing landscape. Hama Rikyū-en is one of the stops on the Sumida River waterbus cruise (*see* panel, page 55). For another, smaller garden try Kyū Shiba Rikyū-en, directly opposite Hamamatsuchō. Both gardens are open from 09:00–17:00 daily.

TOKYO FOR FREE

Views: of the city from the 45th floor of the main Tokyo Metropolitan Government Building (*see* page 98), and from the 38th and 39th floors of Ebisu Garden Place Tower (*see* page 80); of Rainbow Bridge shore line: from Decks Shopping Mall, Odaiba. To see the latest teenage fashion crazes go to Harajuku on Sunday afternoons.
Freebies: tissues handed out on the street for advertising purposes; free food samples in department stores.
Other experiences: Sony Building (*see* page 63) where you can try out Japan's latest high-tech gadgets; also Yebisu Beer Museum (*see* page 80) for history, but not free tasting.

Below: *Hama Rikyū-en is one of Tokyo's most charming havens on the Sumida River.*

5
Tokyo Bay and South Tokyo

Tokyo Bay has played a pivotal role in Japan's history, for here, in 1853, Commodore Perry ended Japan's centuries of self-imposed isolation, and on 2 September 1945, Japan surrendered to **General MacArthur** onboard the USS Missouri.

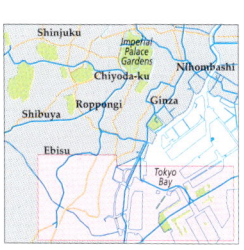

Now the Bay is home to **Virtual Tokyo**, a city firmly rooted in the 21st century, though its origins lie in the froth of the 1980s bubble era, when companies began selling off idle land at vastly inflated prices: down came a skyline of industrial eyesores and up went a series of architectural showpieces on ever-expanding reaches of reclaimed land. An excursion from Shimbashi on the unmanned Yurikamome monorail to the world of **Fuji TV** and **Palette Town** is like a 21st-century journey through *Alice in Wonderland*, where curious monuments are connected by wild-flower promenades.

Shinagawa was a major post-station in the Edo Period, and remains a big transportation centre. Though not the most inspiring area of the city, the southern loop of the Yamanote line between Shinagawa and Gotanda encompasses a few notable sights: **Sengaku-ji**, the burial site of the legendary 47 *rōnin* (*see* page 74); the **Hatakeyama Memorial Museum**, and the **Hara Museum of Contemporary Art**. Also, Meguro, the next stop west of Gotanda, is both a pleasant residential district and home to the **National Park for Nature Study** as well as the Art Deco-style **Tokyo Metropolitan Teien Art Museum** and **Tennonzan Gohyaku Rakan-ji**, a temple with a remarkable display of over 300 carved Buddhist statues.

DON'T MISS

*** Fuji TV Building: space-station architecture.
** Palette Town: chic shopping at VenusFort.
** Hara Museum of Contemporary Art: modern art; attractive lunch venue.
** Sengaku-ji: burial site of the legendary 47 *rōnin*.
** Meguro Temple Tour: stunning sculptures at Gohyaku-ji.
** Tokyo Metropolitan Teien Art Museum: great Art-Deco setting.
* National Park for Nature Study: large park with trees that are over 500 years old.

Opposite: *The Fuji TV building epitomizes Tokyo-Bay architecture.*

Below: *Not New York, but Tokyo Bay: the Statue of Liberty and Rainbow Bridge.*

TOKYO BAY

The best way to see the sights of Tokyo Bay is to buy a day pass on the computerized **Yurikamome line** and stop off at any of its 11 stations. In good weather it is also worth walking between the sights, some of which are relatively close together.

The journey from Shimbashi to Ariake takes 23 minutes. Takeshiba, Hinode and Shibaura-Futō stations on the 'mainland side' of Tokyo Bay hold little interest, although you can get off at Hinode to take the **waterbus** (*see* panel, page 55), which ferries regularly between Hinode Pier and Tokyo Big Sight / Palette Town as well as Fune-no-Kagakukan (Museum of Maritime Science). You can also get off at Shibaura-Futō to walk across **Rainbow Bridge**, named after its multicoloured floodlighting at night. The bridge carries eight lanes of traffic and is open to pedestrians 09:00–21:00 April–October and 10:00–18:00 November–March. There is a charge to use the elevator to the walkway and you must enter 30 minutes before closing.

The next stop is **Odaiba Kaihin Kōen** (Marine Park), where gun emplacements were built in the 1850s during the nervy years of foreign encroachment by Commodore Perry and others. Two of the *daiba* (batteries) remain. Now, the park even boasts its very own mini Statue of Liberty donated by France. There is also a beach, where children can play in specially imported sand against the impressive backdrop of Rainbow Bridge.

The terrace of **Decks Tokyo Beach** is a pleasant place for a drink, though weekends – like everywhere in Tokyo – tend to be crowded. On the third to fifth floors of Decks is a **Joyopolis**, a virtual reality arcade open 10:00–23:00.

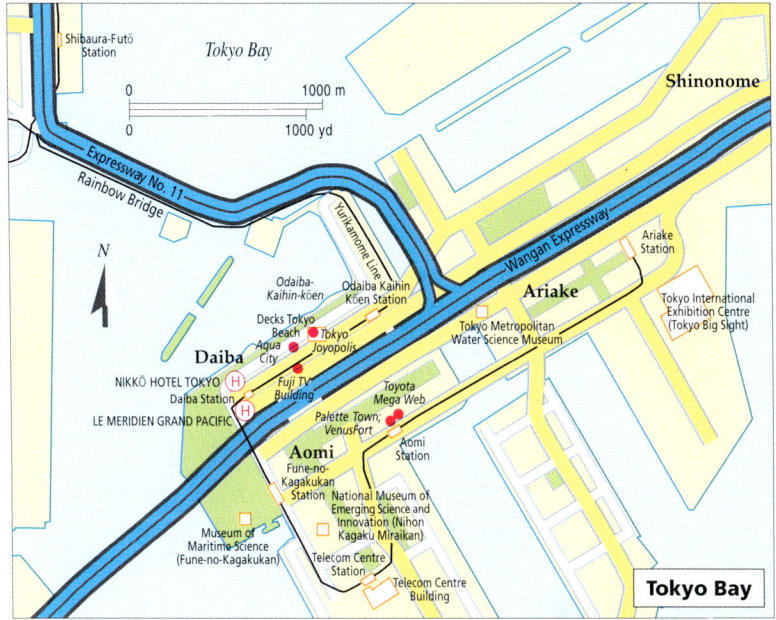

The 6th and 7th floors are home to **Little Hong Kong**. Here are Chinese restaurants where you can snack on *dim sum* (savoury dumplings) and seafood, as well as shops where you can buy a range of Chinese goods. **Aqua City**, next door, is another shopping, restaurant and amusement complex. On the fourth floor is the **Tezuka Osamu World Art Square** devoted to the cartoonist who inspired Japan's modern *manga* business (*see* opposite panel).

Towards Daiba station are the Nikkō Hotel Tokyo and the Le Meridien Grand Pacific, both of which have restaurants with commanding views.

Fuji TV Building ***

Opposite Decks Tokyo Beach is one of Tokyo's most striking buildings designed by the prolific **Tange Kenzō**. From the outside, Fuji TV's shiny metallic headquarters completed in 1996 looks like a gigantic TV set. Within, it

houses a media tower, an office tower and 10 studios, not to mention the 32m (105ft) diameter titanium-panelled observatory sphere, which is well worth visiting for the views. Open from 10:00–21:00 April–October, 10:00–18:00 November–March. (Admission fee charged for observatory.)

Fune-no-Kagakukan (Museum of Maritime Science) ★★

This museum is on board a moored ocean liner and is a good family destination. It has interesting videos, exhibits and interactive displays that explain the **history of shipping**, as well as models of the battleship *Yamato*, and the *Mauritania*. For an additional admission charge you can also view the *Soya*, built in 1938 as a cargo ship for deployment in Antarctica, and the *Yotei-maru*, a ferry that used to sail between Honshū and Hokkaidō. Open 10:00–17:00 daily; until 18:00 on weekends and holidays.

Five minutes' walk from Fune-no-Kagakukan station is Tokyo's newest high-tech museum, the **Nihon Kagaku Miraikan** (National Museum of Emerging Science and Innovation). This concentrates on grown-up topics such as the global environment and life sciences, and is unlikely to prove much fun for children. Open from 10:00–17:00 Wednesday–Monday; until 18:00 on Saturdays July–August. See www.miraikan.jst.go.jp Much more fun is the **Tokyo Metropolitan Water Science Museum**, which offers, among other things, virtual river rides. Open 09:30–17:00 Tuesday–Sunday. Admission free. Closest station: Kokusai Tenjijō Seimon-mae.

After passing a blue space-station construction called **Telecom Centre Building** (possibly one of Japan's most expensive white elephants yet) the Yurikamome line arrives at Aomi station, the stop for Palette Town.

Palette Town ★★

Palette Town is a shopping and restaurant complex whose principal attraction is **VenusFort**, an extraordinary shopping mall in a fake 18th-century Palazzo setting, which owes more to Las Vegas than to Rome. Under a computer-controlled, sky-painted ceiling, which changes at regular intervals from dawn to dusk, Japanese women come here to shop until they drop in their very own designer-boutique theme park, complete with around 160 stores, restaurants and cafés. VenusFort is a good escape on a rainy day. Shops open 11:00–21:00 daily; restaurants usually operate until 23:00.

Also in Palette Town are the Mega Web, a huge Toyota showroom, and **History Garage**, where you can view a range of vintage cars. One of the other attractions is a monumental **Ferris Wheel**.

Tokyo International Exhibition Centre (Tokyo Big Sight) ★

The penultimate stop on the Yurikamome line is Kokusai Tenji-jō Seimon-mae, home to the Tokyo International Exhibition Centre, or Tokyo Big Sight, as it is more commonly known. Completed in 1996, this is Tokyo's biggest conference and trade exhibition venue, instantly recognizable by the gigantic sculpture of a **red-handled saw**, which plunges into the ground in front of the building. There is little reason to linger unless you are attending a conference; the complex's four **inverted pyramids**

Opposite: *At 14m (46ft), this 'Saw, sawing' sculpture is built to withstand earthquakes and high winds.*
Below: *Tokyo Big Sight is the city's premier convention centre.*

and acres of glass are worth casting an eye over for its glorious testimony to bubble-era spending, when money was simply no object.

From the last stop at Ariake, the Yurikamome line retraces its way back to Shimbashi.

FROM SHINAGAWA TO MEGURO

Shinagawa has seen many incarnations in its 400-year history: from a rural post station in the Edo Period it developed into a major *geisha* centre for samurai and wayfarers before disappearing in a cloud of industrial smoke in the early 20th century and eventually reemerging as a first-class hotel, embassy and transportation hub.

Meguro has several memorable **temples** and the outstanding **Tokyo Metropolitan Teien Art Museum**. Its other claims to fame include a **love hotel** built like a castle, and **Meguro Gajo-en**, a prime wedding venue. It also has a couple of museums of limited interest: the bizarre **Meguro Kiseichukan** (Parasite Museum), which has a collection of 45,000 parasites, among them a 8.8m (29ft) tapeworm (open 10:00–17:00, Tuesday–Sunday), and the **Kume Art Museum** in the Kume Building on the west side of Meguro station, which exhibits the works of Kume Keiichirō (1866–1934), Japan's first impressionist painter. Open 10:00–17:00 Thursday–Tuesday.

Below: *Sengaku-ji is famous as the burial site of the 47* rōnin.

Sengaku-ji **

Though by no means Tokyo's most impressive temple, Sengaku-ji is embedded in the Japanese psyche as the

final resting place of the 47 *rōnin* (masterless samurai) who, in 1703, avenged their lord's disgrace by committing collective suicide. Incense hangs thick in the air over the tombs, where people pay their respects daily. In the **Gishikan** (Hall of Loyal Retainers) is a somewhat spooky array of relics from chain mail and armour to fans and doll-representations of the *rōnin*. *Ako Gishi-sai* (memorial celebrations) for the *rōnin* are held at Sengaku-ji on 14 and 15 December. Events include costumed processions and drumming.

Hara Museum of Contemporary Art **

The somewhat dowdy exterior of this 1930s Bauhaus-style building in a quiet side street of Shinagawa masks an elegant interior, which houses a permanent collection of post-1950 works by artists such as Andy Warhol and Roy Lichtenstein, and also stages special exhibitions. The Café d'Art (open 11:00–16:00) designed by Arata Isozaki is a particularly pleasant place for lunch. See www. haramuseum.or.jp for exhibition details. Open 11:00–17:00 Tuesday–Sunday, until 20:00 on Wednesdays. 4–7–25 Kitashinagawa, Shinagawa-ku. Closest station: Shinagawa, Yamanote line.

Hatakeyama Memorial Museum **

This top quality **Japanese art** collection of Nō costumes, tea wares, scrolls and paintings was formed by Hatakeyama Issei (1881–1971), founder of Ebara Corporation, an engineering company. The works are housed in the secluded setting of an old feudal estate, where the Emperor Meiji came to view a Nō performance in 1880. This is one of Tokyo's treats situated far from the madding crowd. English language labelling is reasonable. Shoes must be taken off. Open from 10:00–17:00 Tuesday–Sunday (until 16:30 October–March),

---

SEASONAL FLOWERS

February–March: plum
March–April: camellia, cherry, magnolia
May–June: azalea, wisteria, peony, iris, hydrangea, water lily
July: lotus
September: bush clover
October: maple leaves
November: chrysanthemum

Above: *Japan has over 2.5 million beverage vending machines.*

2–20–12 Shiroganedai, Minato-ku. The closest station: Takanawadai, Asakusa line.

Meguro Temple Tour **

Daien-ji, five minutes from Meguro station down Gyōninzaka, is a charming backwater with an infamous past. One night in 1772, one of Edo's three great fires broke out here, burning one-third of the capital to the ground over the next three days and nights. Daien-ji is known for its 500 small stone *rakan* (Buddha's disciples), all carved with individual expressions. The signs ask you to offer water to the statues to appease the souls of those who died.

A set of much larger statues awaits at **Tennonzan Gohyaku Rakan-ji**, tucked away in the back streets a few minutes walk from Daien-ji. Gohyaku-ji, as the temple is known for short ('The Temple of 500'), originally housed 500 17th-century statues of Buddha's disciples. In 1981 a new hall was completed to house the 305 statues that remain. These finely crafted figures, designated as one of Tokyo's important cultural assets, are the capital's answer to the 1001 images of Kannon at Sanjūsangen-dō in Kyoto.

Close by, along a shopping arcade, is the delightful **Meguro Fudō-son**, which is particularly prettily framed by cherry blossoms in spring. The temple flourished during the Edo Period, when Meguro was a popular pilgrimage site on the edge of Edo. It still retains a village-like atmosphere.

Tokyo Metropolitan Teien Art Museum **
This former home of Prince Asaka (a grandson of Emperor Meiji) was completed in 1933. Designed by

Henri Rapin (1873–1939), the building is a striking amalgam of Art Deco and Imperial Household taste that harks back to Japan's flirtation with intellectualism in the Taisho Period (1912–26). Exhibitions range from paintings to ceramics and sculpture. Open 10:00–18:00 daily, except the second and fourth Wednesdays. 5-21-9 Shiroganedai, Minato-ku. Closest station: Meguro, Yamanote line. Admission to the garden can be obtained separately from the museum. See www. teien-art-museum.ne.jp

Shizen Kyōiku-en (National Park for Nature Study) *
Next door to the Teien Art Museum, the National Park for Nature Study is one of Tokyo's hallowed green spaces and the last bastion of natural life on the Musashino Plateau (*see* page 6). Over 8000 trees cover the park's 20ha (50 acres), which also host rich bird and insect life. The grounds are particularly popular in spring and autumn. Open 09:00–16:00 Tuesday–Sunday, until 17:00 May–August. There is an admission fee and ribbons are handed out. Only 300 ribbons are issued at any one time to contain numbers of visitors.

Matsuoka Museum of Art **
Newly relocated from its former home in Shimbashi, the Matsuoka Museum is yet another exquisite collection of Chinese ceramics as well as Buddhist and Greek, Roman and Egyptian sculpture built up by Matsuoka Seiji, a property developer. Open 10:00–17:00 Tuesday–Sunday. 5-12-6 Shiroganedai, Minato-ku. The closest station: Shirokanedai, Namboku/Tōei Mita line.

Below: *Guests try not to be seen leaving love hotels.*

6
Cool Tokyo

Whatever your age, you will probably feel like last century's vintage among the legions of young Japanese setting Tokyo's fashion and lifestyle trends along the western edge of the Yamanote line, where teenagers get off at Harajuku to cut their teeth on the cute and the trendy before graduating to Ebisu, Shibuya and Shinjuku.

Cool Tokyo starts in Ebisu, where you can experience one of the best city views from the top of **Ebisu Garden Place Tower** before progressing to the ultimate in chic boutiques in neighbouring **Daikanyama**.

Shibuya is a top shopping, clubbing and cultural Mecca where love hotels mingle with eccentric coffee shops such as **The Lion**. Here also is the **Toguri Museum of Art**, one of Tokyo's top Oriental porcelain collections, and, in Komaba, the **Mingeikan**, which displays traditional Japanese folk art.

North and east of the tracks from Shibuya and further on towards Shinjuku is the golden triangle of **Harajuku**, **Omotesandō** and **Aoyama**, where teenagers, the young business set and the forty-somethings all have their respective playgrounds. To sit at one of the ubiquitous cafés and watch the Japanese worship at the altar of fashion and consumerism can be intriguing entertainment in itself.

Roppongi is still a prime Tokyo nightlife ghetto, steamy rather than cool, with a huge range of restaurants, bars, and discos for those in search of sex and sin in varying quantities.

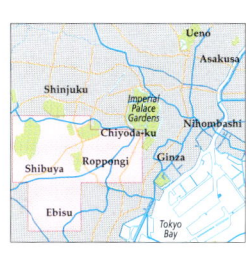

DON'T MISS

*** **Meiji Jingū and Gardens:** an oasis of calm.
*** **From Harajuku to Omotesandō:** top shopping and teenager-watching.
*** **Nezu Institute of Fine Arts:** excellent Asian arts and a wonderful garden.
*** **Daikanyama:** chic boutiques and cafés.
** **Ebisu Garden Place:** a sophisticated experience.
** **Ōta Memorial Museum of Art:** top *ukiyo-e* (woodblock print) collection.
** **Toguri Museum of Art:** the finest oriental porcelain.

Opposite: *Teenagers demonstrate wild fashions at Harajuku.*

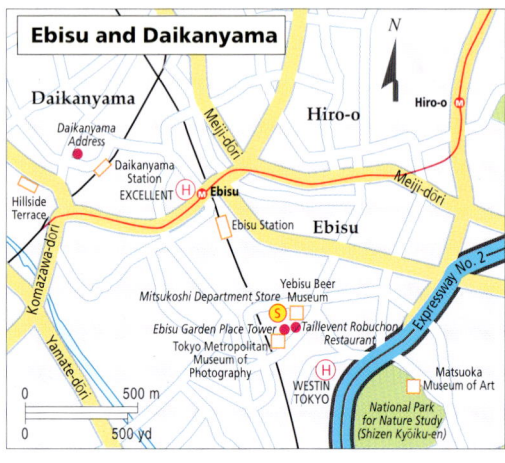

Ebisu and Daikanyama

EBISU AND DAIKANYAMA

Ebisu (sometimes spelt 'Yebisu'), one stop north of Meguro on the Yamanote line, is a station with two very different façades: west of the tracks, the streets are still narrow, packed with small eateries, many of them ramen restaurants; to the east, via the 'Yebisu Skywalk' is one of Tokyo's 'coolest' developments: **Ebisu Garden Place**, a spacious

Opposite: Ebisu Garden Place thrives on its faux-European elegance.

shopping and hotel complex. Another cool spot, between Ebisu and Shibuya, is the café and fashion Mecca of Daikanyama, which has come a long way since the destruction of the Great Kanto Earthquake in 1923.

Ebisu Garden Place ★★

Built on the old Yebisu Brewery site, Ebisu Garden Place is like a grown-up global theme park, offering both fake European and neo-Meiji-Period 'bricktown' architecture, dotted with sculptures ranging from works by Rodin to the 'Flying Croissant'.

The central square is flanked on the left by **Mitsukoshi** department store (an unprepossessing monument to urban taste), a cinema complex and the Yebisu Garden Terrace. On the right is a beer hall and the **Garden Place Tower**, which offers some of the best free views of Tokyo from the 38th and 39th floors, as well as a good range of restaurants. Ahead, the façade of the highly expensive Château Restaurant Taillevent Robuchon offers a virtual glimpse of Paris. Beyond lies The **Westin Tokyo**, one of the city's most luxurious and pleasantly located hotels.

Yebisu Beer Museum behind Mitsukoshi is a high-tech, airy place to spend a few minutes absorbing the history of brewing and viewing some interesting old advertising posters. Open 10:00–18:00 Tuesday–Sunday. Admission free (but not the Tasting Lounge).

Tokyo Metropolitan Museum of Photography **

This excellent museum has a permanent collection of around 18,000 photographs ranging from 19th-century works by Felix Beato and Lewis Carroll to contemporary Japanese photographers. The collection is rotated regularly in imaginative exhibitions. The basement is devoted to a history of the moving image. Open 10:00–18:00 Tuesday–Sunday; until 20:00 Thursday–Friday.

Daikanyama ***

Combining the funkiest and most chic architecture and merchandise – symbolized by the area's gigantic sunflower sculpture – Daikanyama creates its own original atmosphere, far from the computer-controlled environment of VenusFort in Tokyo Bay.

JIYŪGAOKA

Six stops from Shibuya station on the Tōyōko line bound for Yokohama is Jiyūgaoka (Freedom Hill), yet another of Tokyo's cool spots that since the late 1980s has developed into a village-style enclave of hair salons and minimalist chic epitomized by the Ernest Hemingway lifestyle store of linen and cotton wear. Jiyūgaoka is also a 21st-century version of Kappabashi (see page 51), where international designer kitchenware and china prevail rather than utilitarian rice steamers and rice bowls.

Dominating the station area is **Hillside Terrace**, masterminded by the 'Metabolist' architect Maki Fumihiko (*see* page 24). This award-winning development characterized by steel, glass, imaginative tiling and airy spaces began in 1968 and continued for 25 years. The buildings, labelled from A to G, flank Kyūyamate-dōri. Daikanyama bursts with galleries, florists, boutiques, designer names, accessories and retro. Try Café Michelangelo or Café Artifagose for a spot of people watching. Fashion shops range from Jean-Paul Gaultier to High Standard, which sells second-hand clothes.

SHIBUYA

Shibuya station is not as confusing as Shinjuku station, but still takes some navigation: here the Yamanote, Tōyōko and Inokashira lines, as well as the Ginza and Hanzōmon subway lines, all converge. Take a deep breath before joining the weekend stampede across Shibuya crossing headed by the teenage blonde-haired, mobile-phone brigade. Whereas the grandmothers of this generation once shuffled along on wooden *geta* (sandals), these youngsters balance precariously on platform shoes.

Shibuya's most interesting spots are west of the Yamanote line tracks. Orientate yourself by heading for the Hachiko exit and look for the cylindrical **Shibuya 109 Building** on the opposite side of the crossing where Dōgenzaka and Bunkamura–dōri diverge to the left and right respectively.

Below: *Crowds stream across Shibuya crossing every time the lights change.*

In the backstreets up Dōgenzaka – so named after a highwayman who robbed travellers here in the 13th century – is a mass of bars, small restaurants and love hotels lurking behind exteriors ranging from exotic Italian to Japanese 'cute'. The prize for the most unusual café in this area goes to

Left: *The 109 Building in Shibuya is both a useful landmark and a fashion Mecca for young Japanese.*

The Lion (*see* At a Glance, page 120), which plays classical music in a dimly lit church-like interior and expects its customers to listen, not chatter. In short, Dōgenzaka is full of surprises, though these days you are no longer likely to be hijacked.

Other diversions include the **Goto Planetarium** (open 10:00–18:00 Tuesday–Sunday) and Mark City, a new shopping complex.

The road to the right of the 109 Building leads to **Bunkamura** (Culture Village), a cinema, theatre, concert hall, restaurant and shopping complex. On Bunkamura-dōri, just behind the 109 Building, is **Kujiraya**, a whale restaurant where the environmentally cavalier can eat blubber to their hearts' content. (Japan still catches whales for 'research purposes'. According to the Japanese Whaling Association, depriving the Japanese of

---

SMOKING

Like it or not, tobacco fumes are hard to get away from in Japan, where over 50 per cent of men and over 15 per cent of women smoke. Although the Ministry of Health, Labour and Welfare would like to strengthen health warnings and cut smoking disease-related costs, tobacco remains a big earner for the Ministry of Finance. Smoking on international air routes was banned by Japanese airlines only in 1999. All Shinkansen and JR trains have separate non-smoking cars and smoking on the subway system is banned. The situation is less favourable when eating out: few restaurants have effective no-smoking areas.

Above: *The TEPCO Museum consumes less energy than shopping.*

whale meat would be like asking the English to stop eating fish and chips.) Virtually opposite Bunkamura, on the right, is Book 1st, a major bookstore. Beyond Bunkamura is Shōtō, an exclusive residential district on the site of former tea plantations.

Behind Seibu department store, between Inokashira-dōri and Kōen-dōri, is **Parco**, a clothing store complex divided into several buildings, including Club Quattro Shibuya, a concert hall. The latest addition, Zerogate, is just behind **Spain-dōri**, a narrow, hilly lane of cute boutiques and coffee shops mildly reminiscent of the Spanish Steps in Rome, but named after the Spanish-style shop façades initiated by a local owner. At the top of Spain-dōri is **Cinema Rise**, one of Tokyo's few remaining independent cinemas. Another long-established Shibuya shopping institution on Inokashira-dōri is **Tōkyū Hands**, a 'Creative Life Store' selling everything from designer doormats to drills.

Opposite the Tōbu Hotel on Kōen-dōri en route to NHK Broadcasting Centre is the **Tobacco and Salt Museum**, devoted to two of Japan's former state monopolies. Displays trace the development of the worldwide tobacco trade – very important to this nation of inveterate smokers – and salt production. Open Tuesday–Sunday 10:00–18:00. Another dull-sounding, but reasonably entertaining museum five minutes walk away (near Tower Records) is the popular **TEPCO Electric Energy Museum**, instantly recognizable by its silver dome. Seven floors of interactive displays and computer games are devoted to explaining electricity and energy usage. There is virtually no labelling in English. Open 10:30–18:30 Thursday–Tuesday. Admission free.

Toguri Museum of Art **

Situated behind Bunkamura in Shibuya, the Toguri Museum is one of Tokyo's top private collections of Japanese and Chinese porcelain, renowned particularly for its 17th-century Imari and Nabeshima wares. Works are rotated in four exhibitions a year. Open 09:30–17:30 Tuesday–Sunday.

Nihon Mingeikan (Japan Folkcrafts Museum) **

Just beyond Shibuya, in Komaba, this tranquil building with dark wooden interiors was opened in 1936 by **Yanagi Sōetsu** (1889–1961). Yanagi was a leading proponent of *mingei* (folk crafts), which he defined as simple everyday items made by anonymous craftsmen. The collection comprises pottery, textiles, lacquer and woodwork, as well as Korean ceramics, which inspired Yanagi's taste. The only drawback is the lack of English labelling, though most objects speak for themselves. Open 10:00–17:00 Tuesday–Sunday. Closest station: Komaba Tōdaimae, Inokashira line.

HARAJUKU, OMOTESANDŌ AND AOYAMA

The small wooden building of Harajuku station, with its clock tower dating from 1924, stands in calm contrast to the waves of 21st-century urban teenagers surging through Takeshita-dōri, which starts opposite the station and runs parallel with Omotesandō to Meiji-dōri. From a glimpse of Shinto ritual at the Meiji Jingū to shopping and ogling, this corner of Tokyo is a lot of fun.

COFFEE MANIA

The independent *kissaten* (coffee shop) was a once sacred institution where workers could steal a few minutes over a bland cup of 'blendo' coffee. Like the rest of the world, however, Japan has now succumbed to a caffeine tidal wave spear-headed by self-service coffee chains such as Starbucks, Best and Segafredo, which all now compete with Doutor for prime sites. Doutor is Japan's very own coffee chain that first brought reasonably priced coffee to the land of green tea and has its own flagship establishment at Ginza Yon-chome crossing. Starbucks' Shibuya outlet is reputedly the busiest Starbucks branch in the world.

Below: *Omotesandō has plenty of coffee shops.*

Harajuku ***

Takeshita-dōri is at the cutting edge of teenage fashion from Hello Kitty crêpes to leather jackets and polka-dot padded bras. Within the square area bounded by Omotesandō and Takeshita-dōri are a number of back streets with quirky galleries and shops. **Aux Bacchanales**, on Meiji-dōri just past the intersection with Takeshita-dōri, is a good spot to watch the world go by. The nearby Tōgō Shrine, dedicated to Admiral Tōgō, who achieved victory in the Russo-Japanese war of 1904–05, is a popular flea market venue on the first and fourth Sundays of the month (*see* page 28).

Below: *Teenagers strut their retro and fantasy fashions on Sundays by the entrance to the Meiji Jingū.*

Ōta Memorial Museum of Art **

To get away from the teenagers, try the **Ōta Memorial Museum of Art** behind the Laforet Building on Meiji-dōri. This haven of serenity displays, in themed exhibitions, some of the 12,000 Edo-Period *ukiyo-e* (*see* panel, page 61) collected by Ōta Seizō, an insurance industry magnate. Here you get the chance to look at Tokyo the way it used to be. Open 10:30–17:30 Tuesday–Sunday. Shoes off.

Meiji Jingū ***

If you have only one hour for a stroll in Tokyo, go to the **Meiji Jingū** (Shrine). The area approaching the great *torii* (Shinto shrine gateway) provides added fashion entertainment on Sundays when teenagers

Shibuya, Harajuku and Aoyama

Sangūbashi Station
Meiji Jingū Hōmotsuden (Treasure Museum)
Sendagaya
Shinanomachi Station
Kokuritsu-kyogijo

Meiji Jingū Inner Garden

N

Meiji Jingū Iris Garden

Meiji Jingū Outer Garden

0 — 500 m
0 — 500 yd

Yoyogi Park

Tōgō Shrine
Shibuya-ku
Takeshita-dōri
Harajuku Station

National Stadium

Jingū Stadium

Aoyama-itchome

Omotesandō-dōri

Meiji-jingūmae

Ōta Memorial Museum of Art

Watari-Um Contemporary Art Museum
Kyūten-dōri

Gaiemmae

Minami-Aoyama

TO NOGI-JINJA (SHRINE)
Gaien-Higashi-dōri

Zenkoku Dentōteki Kōgeihin (Japan Traditional Crafts Centre)

NHK Broadcasting Centre
Inokashira-dōri

Omotesandō-dōri
Oriental Bazaar
Tokyo Union Church
Omotesandō

Aoyama Cemetery

Nogizaka

TEPCO Electric Energy Museum
Kien-dōri
TŌBU
Hanae Mori Building
Omotesandō

Tokyo University

Kinokuniya Supermarket
Gaien-Nishi-dōri

Toguri Museum of Art
Tōkyū Hands
Tobacco and Salt Museum
United Nations University
Spiral Building

TO NIHON MINGEIKAN (JAPAN FOLKCRAFTS MUSEUM)

Parco
Kodomo no Shiro (National Children's Castle)

Nezu Institute of Fine Arts

Shōtō
Bunkamura
Bunkamura
Seibu
Shibuya 109 Building
Bunkamura-dōri
Shibuya
Shibuya
Goto Planetarium
Shibuya

Dōgenzaka
Shibuya
Shibuya Station
Expressway No. 3

Nishi-Azabu

---

come to parade their latest wild hair-dos and retro or fantasy fashion in the shadow of Tange Kenzō's 1964 Olympic Stadium.

Beyond the great *torii*, along cool, tree-lined avenues you eventually come to the Shrine dedicated to the memories of Emperor Meiji and Empress Shōken. The present Shrine was rebuilt in 1958 after being destroyed in World War II. On weekends it is always worth waiting to glimpse one of the Shrine's many traditional **marriage ceremonies**. The sight of bride and groom being led across the courtyard by a wand-waving Shintō priest is a flashback to Japan's courtly traditions.

At New Year the crowds descend, but weekdays can be truly tranquil. The **Iris Garden**, off the main path en route to the Shrine, is particularly beautiful in June when the irises are out. Open 08:00–17:00 daily. Admission charge.

Right: *Traditional wedding ceremony at the Meiji Jingū, with Shinto priests and* miko *(shrine maidens) in Heian-Period costume.*
Opposite: *Despite recession, the Japanese remain inveterate shoppers, always keen for a bargain.*

The **Meiji Jingū Hōmotsuden** (Treasure Museum) at the north end of the Meiji Jingū grounds is an austere, modern Shinto-style building, which displays portraits of Japan's emperors and personal items of Emperor Meiji and Empress Shoken. Though a somewhat lifeless viewing experience, the museum conveys the grandeur of old Japanese imperialism. Open 09:00–16:00 on weekends and public holidays only.

Omotesandō ★★★

Omotesandō runs between Harajuku and Aoyama-dōri. Not sufficiently grand to be compared to the Champs Elysées, it nevertheless remains a firm *gaijin* (foreigner) favourite for its range of shops, cafés and restaurants, which have grown increasingly European in flavour over the years. Walking from Harajuku towards Omotesandō station, landmark coffee shops on the right-hand side include Perbacco!, a chic Italian spot, and **Café de Ropé**, a charmingly shambolic French café.

Further along from unlikely retail neighbours such as Kiddyland and **Dior**, the inimitable **Oriental Bazaar** has been keeping tourists supplied with old ceramics, kimonos, prints and knicknacks for years. Beyond, the Tokyo Union Church nestles between **Louis Vuitton** and Emporio Armani, while Tange Kenzō's Hanae Mori Building rubs shoulders with a classy Shu Uemura cosmetics store. Near Kiddyland, Kyū Shibuya-gawa Yūhodo, a small road paved over the old Shibuya River,

TOKYO FOR CHILDREN

Hanayashiki: old-fashioned amusement park in Asakusa.
Kiddyland (Omotesandō): everything from cute to cutting-edge toys.
Kodomo no Shiro (National Children's Castle) on Aoyama-dōri: an imaginative play venue for youngsters.
Kodomo no Hi (Children's Day): a national holiday on 5 May marked by the flying of carp banners.
Tokyo Disney Resorts: one of the world's leading amusement complexes (*see* panel, page 72).

winds its way both north and south of Omotesandō, yielding more boutiques and cafés, not to mention hair salons. On weekends, artists and trinket sellers peddle their wares along the length of Omotesandō.

On the left, heading from Harajuku towards Omotesandō crossing, the old **Dōjunkai** apartment buildings dating from 1925 have finally received their death sentence at the hands of Tokyo's redevelopers: they will be replaced by a new residential and commercial building by Ando Tadao due for completion in late 2005.

Nezu Institute of Fine Arts ***

From Omotesandō crossing (with Fuji Bank on your right), Omotesandō-dōri carries on towards Roppongi. About 500m (0.3 miles) from the crossing is the Nezu Institute of Fine Arts. Established in 1940, the institute is a shrine to the eclecticism of its founder, Nezu Kaichirō, whose tastes included ancient **Chinese bronzes** and tea-related objects, ranging from scrolls to ceramics. The collection totals 7000 items, of which seven are National Treasures. Exhibits from the permanent collection are displayed in the Shōwa Gallery; temporary exhibitions are displayed in the Heisei Gallery. For details see www.nezu-muse.or.jp

> **CUTE CHARACTERS**
>
> Japanese *manga* history is full of cute characters, that have spawned merchandising worth billions of dollars. **Hello Kitty!** a pink kitten, created by Sanrio in the 1970s remains a popular figure with little girls, adorning school satchels and mobile phone cases. Other much-loved characters include **Doraemon** a blue robo-cat who possesses a door that takes him anywhere, any time. Though past its peak craze of 1998, **Pokémon** remains big business worldwide. So too, increasingly, is **Yu-Gi-Oh!**, a *manga* world inhabited by Yugi (who becomes Yami Yugi when the 'millennium puzzle' activates his magical powers) and his friends.

The other real attraction is the extensive garden that is dotted with seven teahouses. The Gazebo is a pleasant, if expensive, spot to enjoy a coffee and survey the scene. Open 09:30–16:30 Tuesday–Sunday.

Aoyama *

Aoyama-dōri runs southeast from Shibuya up to Omotesandō and continues northeast to Aoyama-itchōme. Halfway between Shibuya and Omotesandō is **Kodomo no Shiro** (National Children's Castle), one of Tokyo's key attractions for children. This paradise of play, art and music includes a roof garden with jungle

Opposite: *The early bird gets the bargain at Tokyo's flea markets such as this one at Nogi Shrine.*
Right: *From early learning at the National Children's Castle to further learning at the United Nations University (behind).*

gym and ball pools. Open, as a rule, from 12:30–17:30 Tuesday–Friday, 10:00–17:30 on weekends, but times can vary.

Slightly further along on the left is the United Nations University, yet another Tange Kenzō creation. Heading towards Omotesandō crossing, also on the left, is **Kinokuniya Supermarket**, which has been supplying ex-pats with imported goodies for decades; on the right is the distinctive **Spiral Building** by Maki Fumihiko.

Close to the Gaien-nishi-dōri intersection, more or less opposite the Bell Commons fashion complex, is the **Zenkoku Dentōteki Kōgeihin** (Japan Traditional Craft Centre) on the second floor of the Plaza 246 building. Articles ranging from lacquer to baskets and fans are on sale, although the dull atmosphere suggests a museum rather than a shop. Open 10:00–18:00 Friday–Wednesday.

Left along Gaien-nishi-dōri, on the section known as Killer-dōri (supposedly named after its appalling traffic accident record) is the **Watari-Um Contemporary Art Museum**, which features a range of Japanese and international artists. The **On Sundays** shop in the museum building sells a range of T-shirts, postcards, books and stationery. Open 11:00–19:00 Tuesday–Sunday, until 21:00 on Wednesday.

In the other direction along Gaien-nishi-dōri you eventually arrive at the edge of **Aoyama Botchi** (Cemetery), a vast area of graves and cherry trees, where at blossom time, no one has any inhibitions about partying with the dead. A venue worth visiting for its flea markets on the 2nd Sunday of the month is the **Nogi Shrine** dedicated to General Nogi, a hero of the Russo-Japanese War (*see* panel opposite). Closest station: Nogizaka, Chiyoda line.

ROPPONGI

South of Nogizaka, past the Bōeichō (Defence Agency), Tokyo is very much alive and kicking in **High Touch Town**, as Roppongi now calls itself on the bridge over Roppongi Yon-chome crossing, where Gaien-Higashi-dōri and Roppongi-dōri meet. Access to Roppongi has been much improved by the new Namboku line stop at Roppongi-itchōme, not to mention the Ōedo line (Tokyo's new circular sub-way), which now complements the Hibiya line at Roppongi station.

The Americans made this relatively hilly spot their own during the Allied Occupation (1945–52) and ex-pats have come flocking ever since to a dizzying number of restaurants, clubs and bars. Roppongi never shuts: it is effectively one large night club fuelled by expensive alcohol, policed by predominantly black bouncers (not to be argued with), and frequented by enough nationalities to populate the United Nations. As a golden rule, never assume that any bar or night club accepts credit cards.

The oldest institution by Roppongi crossing itself is the all-pink **Almond Café**, by no means the best place for a coffee any more, but a convenient meeting spot. Standing with Almond on your left, Roppongi-dōri heads off towards Nishi Azabu and Shibuya, passing Roppongi 6-chōme on the left, which has now been transformed by the brand-new creation of **Roppongi Hills**, a 11.6ha (27-acre) residential and business complex developed by the Mori Building Company.

The key elements of Roppongi Hills include apart-ments, shops, plazas, a new TV Asahi broadcasting centre and a Grand Hyatt hotel. The top five floors of the

---

THE MORI EMPIRE

In 1959, Mori Taikichirō (1904–93), a professor of economics, founded the Mori Building Company. He never looked back: Mori buildings popped up all over Tokyo bearing the Mori name and a number. The biggest landmark project completed during Mori's lifetime was Ark Hills (1986). When Mori died in 1993 aged 88, *Forbes Magazine* ranked him the wealthiest private citizen in the world. Now his company, under Mori Minoru, continues his legacy of developments such as LaForet Harajuku, VenusFort and Atago Green Hills. Roppongi Hills is Japan's largest private-sector real-estate development to date.

centrepiece 54-storey **Roppongi Tower** house the new **Mori Art Centre**, affiliated with the Metropolitan Museum of Art in New York. According to the architects, the structure of the tower is inspired by Japanese elements such as samurai armour and origami (the folding of paper shapes).

Heading back towards Roppongi crossing, with Almond on your right, turn right at the intersection down Gaien-Higashi-dōri in the direction of Tokyo Tower. Along here you will find all the fast food you want: Starbucks, McDonalds and, behind McDonalds, the Hard Rock Café, immediately recognizable by its model of King Kong. In these back streets there is also **Fukuzushi** (*see* At a Glance, page 120) one of Tokyo's best, most expensive sushi restaurants.

On Gaien-Higashi-dōri the prize for the most original building goes to **Mistral Blue**, a tiny rusting blue New York subway car-turned-bar next to the **Roi Building**, another of Roppongi's landmarks, and home to Paddy Foley's Irish Bar in the basement.

Further along the main drag and off to the left you hit the true low life at **Gas Panic**, which at night is more jammed than the Yamanote line at rush hour (this

---

TŌEI ŌEDO LINE

The 41km (26-mile) Ōedo line, Tokyo's newest subway, was opened in December 2000 at a cost of US$12 billion. Rather like an underground version of the Yamanote line, it circles north from Tochō-mae in Shinjuku around to Kasuga, through the Ueno area out as far as Ryōgoku and Tsukishima before heading back through Roppongi and Aoyama-itchōme. To cheer up the underground experience, many of the 38 stations have been decorated with eye-catching artwork including a gigantic clay fish at Ushigome-Yanagichō station and the phases of the moon at Tsukishima.

Below: *Roppongi Prince Hotel is built around an eye-catching pool.*

JAPANESE TELEVISION

Hopefully you will have better things to do in Tokyo than watch TV, but there is always curiosity value in a small dose. NHK is Japan's equivalent of the BBC, broadcasting the more serious stuff and popular period dramas. In most hotels you can hear the 19:00 NHK news in English by pressing the bilingual button on your TV set. Other channels such as TBS, Fuji TV, Asahi and TV Tokyo all offer a mix of soap operas, sport, game shows and dramas. Top hotels also offer satellite channels such as CNN and BBC World.

will not prevent you being thrown out if you do not have a drink in your hand). Gas Panic is a favourite haunt with US marines.

Slightly more restful than Gas Panic (but not much) is **Geronimo** almost opposite Almond. This bar is frequented by ex-pats late at night downing as many shots as they can. If you suffer from claustrophobia, try the more spacious **Agave**, slightly further on and right. Agave is a Mexican paradise where you can try 400 kinds of tequila and mezcales.

In the distance looms **Tokyo Tower** (*see* panel, page 71), which looks like a piece of outsized Meccano by day, but mildly exotic by night. Not far away in Shiba Kōen is **Zōjō-ji**, once one of Tokyo's guardian temples and a popular place to see in New Year's eve.

AKASAKA

In the opposite direction from Shibuya, Roppongi-dōri heads towards Akasaka, just outside Sotobori–dōri. The area is largely **business** and **embassy-dominated**,

but also a pleasant and convenient place to stay, close both to Roppongi and to central districts such as Kasumigaseki and Yūrakuchō. The hotels that rule the skyline include the Akasaka Prince Hotel, designed by Tange Kenzō, and the older New Ōtani. Nearby is the excellent Suntory Museum of Art (*see* page 35).

ARK Hills (an acronym for Akasaka-Roppongi Knot) is a cool, elegant complex comprising the ANA Hotel, the ARK Tower, offices, restaurants, and Suntory Hall, a prime concert venue. The ARK Hills plaza, complete with fountains, is dedicated to the late conductor Herbert von Karajan. The brand new Roppongi Hills development is twice the size of ARK Hills.

Behind ARK Hills is the **Ōkura Hotel**, the *grande dame* of Tokyo accommodation, nowadays merely one of many five-star competitors.

Ōkura Shūkōkan Museum ✶✶

The Ōkura Hotel boasts what is effectively Japan's first private art museum. This Chinese villa set in a sculpture garden opposite the Ōkura Hotel houses a top-quality display of Oriental fine arts originally collected by Baron Ōkura Kihachiro in the late 19th century. It contains three National Treasures, including a sculpture of Samanthabadra on an elephant, and many other important Japanese and Chinese items. Open 10:00–04:30 Tuesday–Sunday. Admission free to hotel guests.

NHK Broadcast Museum ✶

Near Kamiyachō station, up a flight of stone steps, this quirky, surprisingly old-fashioned museum established in 1956 displays everything from 1920s radios to recordings of NHK soap operas and the equipment used to broadcast the 1964 Olympic Games. A try-out studio allows you to sit at a Shinkansen (bullet train) window with passing scenery and see how newsreaders use teleprompts. The labelling suffers from a disappointing lack of English in comparison with the informative website: www.nhk.or.jp/bunken/museum-en Open 09:30–16.30 Tuesday–Sunday. Admission free.

Above: *The fountain in the Herbert von Karajan Plaza, ARK Hills, provides office workers with respite from the summer heat.*
Opposite: *When completed in 1958, the Tokyo Tower was the tallest self-supporting structure in the world, 13m (43ft) higher than the Eiffel Tower.*

7
From Shinjuku
to Ikebukuro

Like Shinagawa, Shinjuku was a **post station**, which serviced huge numbers of feudal retainers en route to Edo in the 17th and 18th centuries. By the Taishō Period, it was also one of the exit points for the vast amounts of night soil produced by a growing city that had not yet come up with an adequate sewage system. Now it is a thriving city in itself, with the most impressive skyline in all Tokyo, dominated by the **Tokyo Metropolitan Government Building**.

Shinjuku requires rigorous orientation when you exit its mind-numbingly complex station: west is skyscraper city, east is the low life of Kabukichō and Gay Tokyo, and south is the pristine Takashimaya Times Square complex and the attractive **Shinjuku Gyoen** (gardens). Whatever your mission, you will need plenty of stamina.

West of Shinjuku on the Odakyu line is the attractive enclave of **Shimokitazawa** and along the Chūō line, Kichijōji, where artists hang out in Inokashira Park on weekends.

Further east along the Yamanote line is Ikebukuro, home to the rather passé Sunshine City complex and, more interestingly, **Sugamo**, where the older generation get off to shop, gossip and cure their pains at the intriguing temple of **Kōgan-ji**. There are also several worthwhile sights within the northern corner of the Yamanote line such as the temple of **Gokoku-ji** and **Koishikawa Shokubutsu-en**, the botanical gardens of Tokyo University.

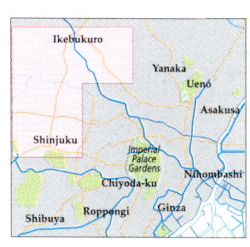

DON'T MISS

*** Tokyo Metropolitan Government Building: the best view of Tokyo.
** Takashimaya Times Square: a pleasant rain-free shopping experience.
** Shinjuku Gyoen: French, English and Japanese gardens.
** Shimokitazawa: from bagels to bars.
** Gokoku-ji: an out-of-the-way temple gem.
** Sugamo: a favourite backwater with the elderly.

Opposite: *The Tokyo Metropolitan Government Buildings tower above Shinjuku.*

Above: *Shinjuku has hundreds of restaurants serving traditional Japanese cuisine, including fugu (blowfish).*

WEST SHINJUKU

West of Shinjuku station, which processes a mind-boggling two million people every day, is the high life, a serene sky-scraper city, whose **Tokyo Metropolitan Government Building** provides the best free views in the city. Virtually the only relic of older days is Shomben Yokochō, unpoetically translated as 'Piss Alley', a narrow street behind Odakyu department store crammed with tiny bars and eateries.

Tokyo Metropolitan Government Building ⋆⋆⋆

Designed by Tange Kenzō, the **Tochō** – as the 400,000m² (480,000 square yard) Tokyo Metropolitan Government complex is commonly known – dominates the Shinjuku skyline. One of the best ways to understand the geography of Shinjuku at a glance is to take the non-stop elevator up one of the twin towers of the main building and look down on the area beneath from the observatory.

To the southwest you will see the distinctive triple-stepped silhouette of **Shinjuku Park Tower**, yet another Tange Kenzō extravaganza, whose top 15 floors are occupied by the Shinjuku Park Hyatt Hotel, and, further away, the 54-storey tower of **Tokyo Opera City**. (If you are really lucky you will see Mount Fuji in the distance. The best months tend to be December–February). To the northeast, the two tallest buildings are the Shinjuku Centre Building and the Sompo Japan Headquarters Building (which flares out towards the base).

Both Tochō towers have observatories on the 45th floor, reached in 55 seconds by express elevator from the 1st floor. At least one observatory is open daily 09:30–22:00. Admission free.

Tōgō Seiji Art Museum *

The core artist of this collection, housed on the 42nd floor of the Sompo Japan (formerly Yasuda Fire and Marine) Headquarters Building in Shinjuku, is Tōgō Seiji, who experimented with Futurism in Europe in the 1920s and is known for his depictions of women. The *pièce de rés-istance* is Van Gogh's 1899 version of **Sunflowers**, bought in 1987 for nearly US$40 million. Sitting in splendid isolation between works by Gaugin and Cézanne (when not on loan), this burst of sunshine is a fitting reminder of the heady days of the 1980s, when money was no object and the sky was the limit. Open 10:00–18:00 (last entry 17:30) Tuesday–Sunday. For exhibition details see www.sompo-japan.co.jp/museum

---

SHINJUKU'S TALLEST SKYSCRAPERS

Tochō No 1 Building: 243m (797ft).
NTT DoCoMo Yoyogi Building: 240m (787ft).
Shinjuku Park Tower: 235m (771ft).
Tokyo Opera City Tower: 234m (768ft).
Shinjuku Centre Building: 223m (732ft).

Tokyo Opera City *

Opened in 1999, the Tokyo Opera City complex includes an impressive art gallery, which displays contemporary artwork from around the world, and a cathedral-like concert hall. For concert and exhibition schedules see www.operacity.jp

The NTT Intercommunications Centre (ICC) on the fourth to sixth floors of the Tokyo City Opera Tower

Below: *The Tokyo Metropolitan Government Buildings (left) and Shinjuku Park Tower (right) dominate West Shinjuku.*

**BEST CHERRY-BLOSSOM
VIEWING SPOTS**

Cherry-blossom viewing is
a quasi-religious ritual that
takes place from late-March–
early-April. In Japanese
literature the cherry blossom
is a symbol of life's brevity;
in real life it provides a good
excuse for office workers and
friends to bond over a beer.
The biggest crowds of
picnickers go to Ueno Park,
the Yasukuni Shrine and
Aoyama Cemetery. The
Chidorigafuchi Moat area
north of the Imperial Palace
also provides a spectacular
concentration of blossoms,
as does Shinjuku Gyoen. To
avoid the crowds, try less
frequented venues such as
Koishikawa Shokubutsu-en
(see page 106).

Below: *Takashimaya
Times Square in Shinjuku
is one of the world's
biggest department
store buildings.*

displays art that employs electronic technology. Open
10:00–18:00 Tuesday–Sunday. Often closed for unspeci-
fied periods between exhibitions.

EAST SHINJUKU

East of Shinjuku station is **Kabukichō, Golden Gai** and
Shinjuku Ni-chome, heart of **Gay Tokyo**; also on the
east side, but marked as the new south exit of Shinjuku
station, is the road to consumer heaven at Takashimaya
Times Square and, beyond, Shinjuku Gyoen, a garden
where you can draw breath.

The east exit of the station brings you to the big video
screen of Studio Alta. Running to the right, beyond
Sakuraya and **Yodobashi Camera** is Shinjuku-dōri,
home to **Kinokuniya Book Store** (much more cramped
than its newer counterpart annexed to Takashimaya
Times Square), Mitsukoshi, **Isetan** and many other stores
in the Shinjuku San-chome area.

Kabukichō **

Left by Isetan, heading north along Meiji-dōri, and across
Yasukuni-dōri, is the **Hanazono Shrine**, venue of a flea
market on Sundays (*see* panel, page 28). Behind is **Golden
Gai**, a block of Kabukichō-itchōme packed with tiny bars
reminiscent of *shitamachi* areas such as Ueno. Much less
spacious, but just as smoky as the cafés of Paris where
Sartre and his friends would gather, these bars have
served literati, film directors and artists for decades.
Almost all of the bars serve
regulars only. **La Jetée** is
probably the most accept-
ing of unknown *gaijin*.

Shiki no Michi (Four
Seasons Path) behind
Golden Gai leads back
to Yasukuni-dōri, which
forms the boundary of
Kabukichō proper, a teem-
ing mass of karaoke
studios, restaurants, porn

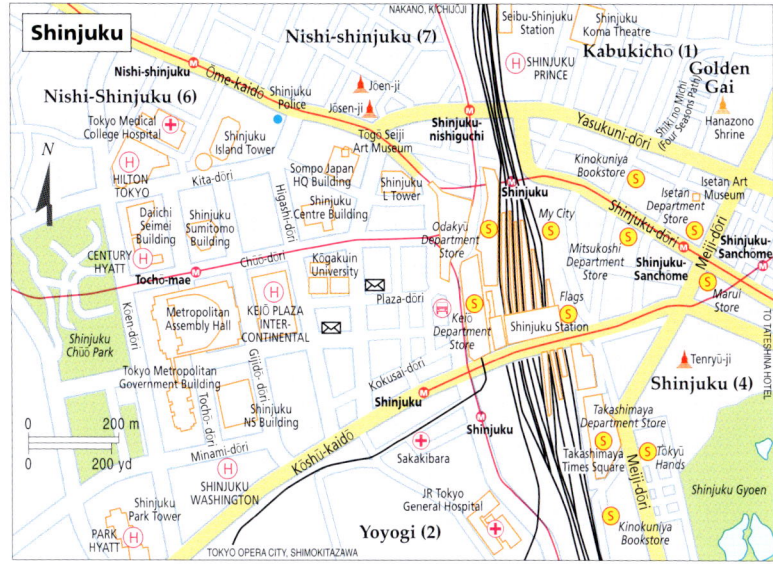

cinemas, strip shows, soaplands (once called Turkish baths, aka brothels, but renamed by request of the Turkish) and peep shows.

Takashimaya Times Square **

Though far removed from the real Times Square in New York, the Takashimaya Times Square Building is flanked by its very own quasi-Empire State Building in the form of an NTT DoCoMo mobile communications tower. It also provides one of the world's largest rain-free shopping experiences, encompassing a branch of **Tōkyū Hands**, an adjoining branch of Kinokuniya bookstore and a whole host of other retail experiences and thirty restaurants. The buildings across the tracks include JR East's headquarters and **Emporio Armani**.

Shinjuku Gyoen **

When the crowds are too much, Shinjuku Gyoen, a former feudal estate that passed into imperial hands in 1906, provides the perfect retreat (except in cherry-blossom season).

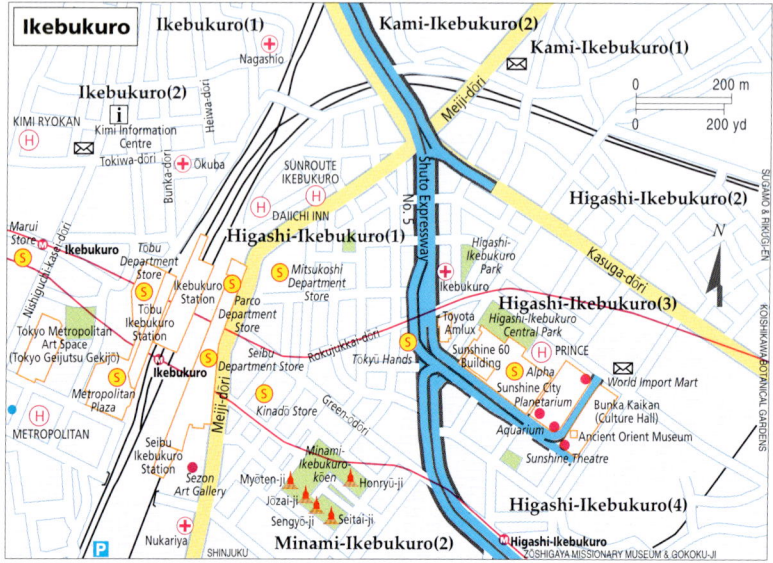

Covering 58ha (144 acres), this highly attractive breath of
Meiji-Period air has formal French, English landscape
and traditional Japanese sections as well as a large
domed greenhouse containing palms and subtropical
species. Open 09:00–16:30 (greenhouse 11:00–15:30)
Tuesday–Sunday, but daily 25 March – 24 April and 1–15
November. The Old Imperial Resthouse is open
10:00–15:00, 2nd and 4th Saturdays of the month only.

WEST OF SHINJUKU

Outside the Yamanote line, beyond Shinjuku and
Shibuya, are several small enclaves that have become
increasingly fashionable over the past few years but
remain relatively unglitzy. West along the orange Chūo
line are Nakano, Kōenji and Kichijō-ji, all of them
younger-generation spots full of restaurants and bars.

Kichijōji *

Eight stops from Shinjuku is **Kichijōji** (also on the
Inokashira line from Shibuya), home to Tower Records,

Starbucks, Parco Books, many eateries and **Inokashira Park**, a popular destination for young families. More infamously the depressive novelist Osamu Dazai and his lover committed suicide here in 1948. The pond in the park functions as a mini nature reserve swarming with carp, as well as a boating venue for courting couples. On weekends there is a quasi-flea market and artists give impromptu performances by the lake.

Shimokitazawa **

Situated on both the Odakyu line from Shinjuku and the Inokashira line from Shibuya, Shimokitazawa is a highly popular residential area, with a laid-back **village atmosphere** shaped by a student presence from the Komaba campus of Tokyo University, only one station away. Wander in any direction either north or south of the Odakyu line and you will not go far wrong among a plethora of shops, bakeries and restaurants, though most of the nightlife is to the south. Some of the tiniest bars imaginable exist here (*see* 'At a Glance' page 121).

IKEBUKURO

Ikebukuro is divided west and east of the railway tracks by the Tōbu and Seibu retail empires respectively. To the east is Sunshine 60 Street, which leads to the 60-storey skyscraper of **Sunshine City**, a complex of four buildings comprising a virtual city within a city on the spot where Class-A war criminals were executed in 1948 at Sugamo Jail.

Though distinctly outside the orbit of Cool Tokyo, Ikebukuro is worth visiting for curiosity value. Development on the Tōbu side is less monolithic than on the

> ### EXECUTIONS IN SUGAMO
>
> Over 100 Class-A war criminal suspects were incarcerated in Sugamo Prison during the war crimes trials following World War II. Twenty-eight were indicted and, on 23 December, 1948, seven were executed, including General Tōjō Hideki, Japan's war time Prime Minister. On the instruction of General MacArthur and his staff, Tōjō and the others did not implicate Emperor Hirohito in atrocities during the trial, a move that aided the General's goal of maintaining the Chrysanthemum Throne as a symbol of continuity into the post-war era. On this occasion, execution rather than ritual suicide became the ultimate test of 'loyalty to the emperor'.

Below: *America captures a corner of the Ikebukuro retail market.*

TŌBU AND SEIBU EMPIRES

Tōbu and Seibu department stores, two of the world's largest, are part of separate businesses encompassing railway lines, property and hotels. These empires were born of intense rivalry between two business magnates, Nezu Kaichirō (1860–1940), founder of the Teikoku Oil Company and the Nezu Institutute of Fine Arts (see page 89), and Tsutsumi Yasujirō (1889–1964). Tsutsumi Yoshiaki (one of Yasujirō's sons) is now the power behind the Seibu empire and remains, reputedly, one of the world's wealthiest people.

Seibu side. The highlight is the **Tokyo Geijutsu Gekijō** (Metropolitan Art Space), an exhibition and concert hall complex enhanced by greenery and waterfalls. Also west of the tracks is Marui department store and the Tōbu Spice Building, which contains a host of restaurants.

On the east side, Sunshine 60 Street offers a plethora of shops and restaurants before you arrive at the Sunshine 60 Building itself, where a dizzyingly fast elevator, complete with elevator girls, takes you up to the observation deck on the 60th floor. These days it is not worth paying the fee given the free views of Tokyo available elsewhere (see page 67). The other three buildings within the complex – all reasonably well signposted in English – are the Prince Hotel, the World Import Mart (a 10-storey building with a planetarium and aquarium on top) and the Bunka Kaikan (Culture Hall).

The **Ancient Orient Museum** on the seventh floor of the Bunka Kaikan has excellent examples of Egyptian and West Asian art from a permanent collection and stages several special exhibitions each year, but virtually nothing is labelled in English. Open 10:00–17:00 daily.

Also on the east side is **Amlux**, a Toyota showroom not to be missed by automobile buffs.

Opposite: *Zōshigaya Missionary Museum is a time capsule of early 20th-century foreign architecture.*
Right: *St Mary's Cathedral is one of Tange Kenzō's typically dramatic early works.*

AROUND IKEBUKURO

Within the northwest corner of the Yamanote line are several sights slightly off the beaten track. One is **St Mary's Cathedral** on Meijirō-dōri. This landmark church is an austere, sweeping fluted sheet of steel reminiscent of the Yoyogi Olympic Stadium, which is hardly surprising given that both buildings were designed by Tange Kenzō and both joined the Tokyo skyline in 1964. The dull concrete interior is the very antithesis of the sun-catching exterior. Closest station: Edogawabashi, Yūrakuchō line.

Opposite the cathedral is the **Chinzan-sō Four Seasons**, one of Tokyo's top hotels and glitziest wedding venues, where Tokyo's young and rich can enjoy their fluffy notions of a white wedding at one of two chapels before changing into traditional dress and posing among the pagodas and gazebos in the stunning gardens that once comprised the estate of Prince Yamagata Aritomo, a Meiji-era statesman. It is worth taking out a small mortgage for a coffee in the Café Foresta, which overlooks the gardens, before taking a short stroll.

Zōshigaya Missionary Museum *

This white and green example of American colonial architecture from 1907 is one of only 20 surviving missionary houses in Japan. It was built for John Moody McCaleb of Nashville, Tennessee, who spent 50 years of his life trying to convert the Japanese to Christianity. The lack of English labelling does not detract from the enjoyment of browsing around this attractive house. Open

> **RECYCLING**
>
> Tokyo produces 40 million tonnes of refuse each year, so it takes recycling very seriously: household waste must be religiously segregated into combustible and non-combustible items. Indeed, foreign residents are severely castigated by their Japanese neighbours if they contravene the regulations. Even hotels are obliged to recycle as much of their kitchen waste as possible. On station platforms you will find different bins for glass, cans and paper: take care to throw your rubbish into the right receptacle.

09:00–16:30 Tuesday–Sunday (closed on the third Sunday of the month). Admission free. 1-25-5 Zōshigaya, Toshima-ku. Closest station: Higashi Ikebukuro, Yūrakuchō line.

Gokoku-ji **

Gokoku-ji is one of Tokyo's out-of-the-way temple gems. The patina of the roof, which echoes the green colour of the steps, is particularly picturesque. The main hall dating from 1697 is an Important Cultural Treasure. Buried in **Zōshigaya Cemetery** adjacent to the temple are several literary figures including the Greco-Irish author Lafcadio Hearn and the Tokyo novelist Nagai Kafū (1879–1959). Closest station: Gokokuji, Yūrakuchō line.

Koishikawa Shokubutsu-en (Botanical Gardens) **

This unmanicured oasis belonging to Tokyo University reflects a real sense of botanical pioneering, though without the grandeur of Kew Gardens. Signs in Japanese proudly claim that the world contains 10,000 plant species, of which Japan has 630 (six per cent) compared with 400 in North America and a mere 140 in Europe.

**LAFCADIO HEARN
(1850–1904)**

Born of a Greek father and Irish mother, Lafcadio Hearn arrived in Japan in 1890 as a correspondent for *Harper's* magazine. He stayed on until his death in 1904, teaching in Tokyo, Matsue, Kumamoto and Kobe. In Matsue, he met and married Koizumi Seto, a samurai's daughter, and changed his name to **Koizumi Yakumo**. Hearn wrote about Japan in sentimental, but sometimes enlightening prose; his books were widely read in the West as the voice of authority on matters Oriental. Hearn taught at both Tokyo and Waseda Universities. He is buried in Zōshigaya Cemetery.

Over an area of 7ha (18 acres), tropical plants mingle happily with wisteria, juniper, cherry and rhododendron. Open 09:00–16:30 Tuesday–Sunday. (Pay the entrance fee at the small shop opposite the entrance.) Closest station, Myōgadani, Marunouchi line.

Sugamo **

Sugamo is where Tokyo's rapidly ageing senior citizens get off the Yamanote line for a shop and a gossip long after they have graduated from the excesses of Shinjuku. Even the **Tōden Arakawa Tram line** that passes through Sugamo en route from Waseda to Minowabashi is a picturesque relic of a bygone age as it rattles along heralded by a clanging bell. It can be very crowded, however, and even octogenarians are not beyond using their elbows to ensure a seat.

From the north exit of the station, on the opposite side of the road, follow the stream of predominantly elderly women down 'Jizō-dōri' arcade lined with stalls and shops selling *sembei* (rice crackers), sweets and woolly jumpers. Past Shinshō-ji (the first temple on the left) is **Kōgan-ji** (further down on the right), where Buddhist monks in conical hats often stand collecting alms. Kōgan-ji is famous for its image of **Togenuki Jizō** (Splinter Removing Jizō). To cure their ills, people queue to wash the part of the statue that corresponds to the location of their own aches and pains.

Rikugi-en **

Last, but far from least, of Tokyo's old gardens is Rikugi-en, a small, attractive blend of woods, water and islands commemorating famous literary scenes. Open 09:00–17:00 daily. Closest station: Komagome, Yamanote line.

> ### THE JAPANESE GARDEN
>
> Green spaces account for only 10 per cent of Tokyo, but provide much needed escape. The art of the garden was born in China and transmitted to Japan via Korea in around the 7th century. By the 16th century the Japanese garden relied on a set of specifically prescribed features: spaciousness, seclusion, an artificial element (bridges or lanterns), an air of antiquity, running water and extensive views. Other commonly found elements include the carp pond and *shishiodoshi* ('deer-scaring device'), a bamboo tube, which, when full of water, tips down on to a stone and gently disturbs the peace.

Opposite: *The Togenuki Jizō statue is a favourite destination for the elderly.*

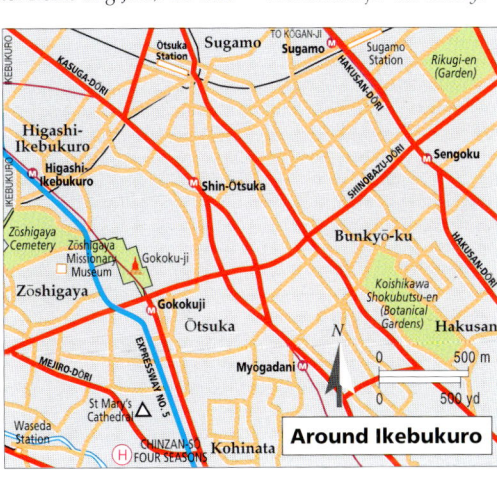

Around Ikebukuro

8
Around Tokyo

Some of Japan's most famous icons lie well within reach of Tokyo by train. First stop westwards is Yokohama, one of Japan's original **Treaty Ports**, so designated in 1858. Although it is the nation's second largest city, **Yokohama** is easier on the eye than Tokyo and has a more relaxed atmosphere: a walk on the Bluff and a meal in Chinatown makes even just a few hours here worthwhile.

More of a tonic still is the small temple town of **Kamakura**, Japan's 13th-century capital, which is easy to see on foot or bicycle. The top attractions are the imposing **Great Buddha** and **Hachiman Shrine**, but there are plenty of much quieter escapes, such as the shady Zen temples of Kita-Kamakura.

For *onsen* (hot-springs) and a dose of nostalgia, head further west to the **Fuji-Hakone-Izu National Park**, for this is the land immortalized in Hokusai's series of wood-block prints entitled *Thirty-six Views of Mount Fuji*. The options include taking the Hakone Cable Car over the malodorous moonscape of Ōwakudani and sailing along **Lake Ashi**, or driving down the **Izu Peninsula** to the historic port of **Shimoda**.

North of Tokyo lies the **Nikkō National Park**, home to **Lake Chūzenji** and the impressive Kegon Falls, not to mention the gaudily sumptuous **Tōshō-gū** (grand mausoleum) of Tokugawa Ieyasu, the *shōgun* who first made Tokyo his capital. Completed in 1636, the Tōshō-gū is Japan's most elaborate piece of chinoiserie. In mid-May and mid-October, sumptuous festivals re-enact the days of the *shōguns*.

Opposite: *Great Buddha (Daibutsu) is one of Japan's most famous images.*

YOKOHAMA

Yokohama's past and future merge spectacularly from the Bluff, where the view of moss-covered graves in the Foreigners' Cemetery gives way to the Minato Mirai waterfront skyline, an ever-evolving world of shopping malls and restaurants focused on the 296m (972ft) **Landmark Tower**, which offers one of the fastest elevator rides in the world.

Chinatown **

Chinatown grew up with the merchants who started trading in Yokohama in the 1870s. At its heart is the gaudy temple of **Guan Yu** (the God of War), which looks highly theatrical illuminated at night. The smokey aroma of roasting ducks and steaming dumplings wafting up from Chinatown's 200 or so restaurants is pure Hong Kong. *Ishikawachō* is the closest JR station for Chinatown, as well as Yamate and Motomachi.

Yamate (The Bluff) **

From boutique-laden **Motomachi** a series of small lanes lead steeply up to Yamate, the area first inhabited by foreign diplomats, architects and engineers. A series of English information boards with area maps in Yamate, Negishi and Honmoku wards make this large area of Yokohama pleasant for a stroll.

Several historic, wooden houses have been preserved in Yamate: admission is free to **Ehrismann's Residence**, the **Bluff 18 Bankan Residence** in the Yamate Italian Garden, the **Diplomat's House** and the recently opened **234 Bankan**. By the **Foreigners' Cemetery**, the last resting place of 4500 people from 40 countries, is the distinctive, turreted **Yamate Jūbankan** – now a French restaurant.

**OFF-BEAT
YOKOHAMA MUSUEMS**

Doll Museum: the ultimate global dolls house with over 9000 examples from 135 countries. By Yamashita-kōen.
Rāmen Museum: a wonderfully wacky place to learn about the history of the noodle and to eat local varieties. Open 11:00–23.00, daily except Tuesday. Shin-Yokohama station.
Silk Museum: from cocoon to kimono, displays on silk production. Open 09:00–16:30 Tuesday–Sunday. By Yamashita-kōen.

KAMAKURA

The warrior **Minamoto Yoritomo** chose this hilly, sea-side town as his capital in 1192. Kamakura has a medieval heritage of 65 temples, 19 shrines and a host of festivals. In spring, the cherry blossoms are sublime; in summer, surfers come flocking to what makes a poor alternative to Hawaii. Either hire a bicycle at the station or just explore on foot. **Komachi-dōri**, parallel with Wakamiya Ōji is fun for its stalls and shops. **Eastern Kamakura** has several small temples off the beaten track, of which **Sugimoto-dera** is the oldest (founded in 734). Perched at the top of a steep flight of steps, it has a chaotic interior, full of chains of paper cranes and dimly lit statues. Meanwhile, **Hōkoku-ji** is justly renowned for its bamboo grove, which evokes all the atmosphere of Kurosawa's film, *Rashōmon*.

Kita-Kamakura **

Kamakura has five major **Zen temples** characterized by a triple-bay gate (*san-mon*) and buildings aligned on a north-south axis: Kenchō-ji, Engaku-ji, Jūfuku-ji Jōchi-ji, and Jōmyō-ji all lie in the hills around Kita-Kamakura, one stop before Kamakura station. A walk through the spacious, cedar-shaded grounds of **Engaku-ji** is a good antidote to Tokyo fatigue. Nearby is **Tōkei-ji** (Divorce

MAIN FESTIVALS

Kamakura Festival, at the Hachiman Shrine, a week from the Sunday closest to April 13, features costumed processions and *yabusame* (mounted archery). Coincides with the cherry-blossom season.
Bon Lantern Festival takes place from 7–9 August at the Hachiman Shrine. Spectacular **fireworks** on 10 August over Sagami Bay.
Autumn Festival takes place from 14–16 September at the Hachiman Shrine. *Yabusame* on the 16th.
Takigi-Nō from 8–9 October at the Kamakura Shrine (Nō drama by torchlight).

Opposite: *The Ferris wheel in front of the 296m (972ft) Landmark Tower in Yokohama dazzles by night.*

Temple) a haven where abused wives could become nuns. The **Ten'en Hiking Course** is a 90-minute trail that loops north from Zuisen-ji (famous for its plum blossoms in February) in the east to **Kenchō-ji** in the west, passing *yagura* (burial caves) in the cliffs. It is a further 2km (1.3 miles) from here to Kamakura's main sites.

Zeniarai Benten (Money-washing Shrine) ***

Zeniarai Benten is Kamakura's quirkiest shrine. Here, at a spring deep within in a cave reached through a succession of *torii* and tunnels, the Japanese religiously wash their money in the hope that **Benten** (Goddess of Fortune) will double its value.

Great Buddha of Kōtoku-in ***

The Great Buddha (**Daibutsu**) is Kamakura's most venerable resident. Completed in 1252, he is a gargantuan 11.5m (38ft) hollow, bronze representation of **Amida Buddha**, who guides believers in Pure Land Buddhism to the Western Paradise. Since 1495, when the roof over his head was last destroyed, he has sat alfresco, having calmly survived all disasters known to man.

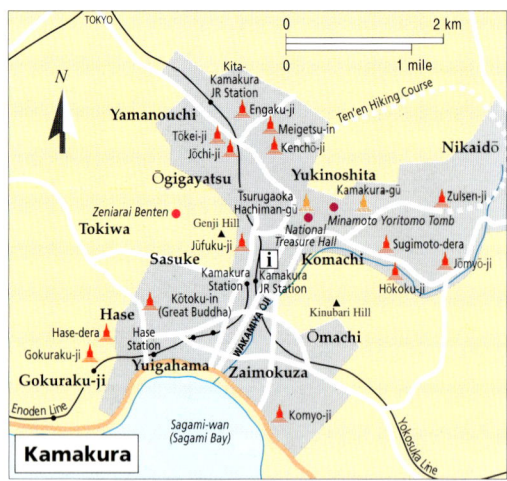

Hase-dera **

Hase-dera has good views across Sagami Bay. It is also home to the 9m (30ft) eleven-headed **Kamakura Kannon** (Goddess of Mercy), reputedly Japan's tallest wooden sculpture, dating from the 8th century. Its saddest inhabitants, however, are hundreds of small stone statues depicting **Jizō** (Saviour of Children). Dressed in bibs and hats, they commemorate the souls of aborted or miscarried babies.

Tsurugaoka Hachiman-gū (Hachiman Shrine) ***

This imposing Minamoto clan shrine is dedicated to **Hachiman** (God of War). In spring and autumn it is the venue of major festivals commemorating Kamakura's rich and often bloodstained past. It is also a favourite blossom-viewing spot.

FUJI-HAKONE-IZU NATIONAL PARK

The snow-crusted volcanic cone of Mount Fuji is deservedly one of the world's most recognizable images. 'No wonder that it is a sacred mountain, and so dear to the Japanese that their art is never weary of representing it,' wrote Isabella Bird, as she sailed into Yokohama in 1878.

Above: *Mt Fuji rises majestically above the sulphurous steam of Ōwakudani.*

Hakone **

In the days of the *shōguns*, Hakone was the site of a major barrier on the **Tōkaidō**, the busiest highway leading to Edo. Evading the checkpost was an invitation to death by crucifixion. Today there is a peril-free, circular tour from the train terminus of Hakone Yumoto by funicular railway, cable car, boat and bus through this quintessential Fuji-viewing region 90km (56 miles) west of Tokyo.

Highlights include **Miyanoshita**, an *onsen* town dominated by the 19th-century **Fujiya Hotel**, and the **Hakone Open Air Museum** (by Chōkoku-no-mori station), which is literally a breath of fresh air for its gardens full of Rodin and Henry Moore sculptures. Open 09:00–17:00 March–October, until 16:00 November–February.

Between Sōunzan and Lake Ashi, a cable car passes over the malodorous moonscape of **Ōwakudani**, where the Japanese love to boil eggs in sulphurous pools; on clear days, Fuji's cone looms through the steam. Down at Lake Ashi, the views are even better; from here a splendidly tacky pirate ship sails south past the picturesque

CLIMBING MOUNT FUJI

Nihon (Japan) means 'origin of the sun', so it is appropriate that the goal of climbing Mount Fuji is to see the sun rise. The climbing season lasts from 1 July – 31 August. 'No sleep – tumult all night of parties returning late from the mountain, or arriving for the pilgrimage,' wrote Lafcadio Hearn from his mountain hut at 03:30 on 25 August 1897. Little has changed. Most people drive up to the 5th station and then walk the remaining six hours to the summit. Climbing Mount Fuji is an institution, not a recipe for enjoyment, although a good sunrise really can make it all worthwhile.

Above: *The vermilion torii of Hakone Shrine by the tranquil waters of Lake Ashi.*

torii of **Hakone Shrine** to the village of Hakone-machi, site of the Tōkaidō barrier. A short walk along an avenue of 17th-century Japanese cedar trees brings you to Moto Hakone, from where buses leave for Hakone Yumoto.

Izu Peninsula **

Hiring a car at Atami is useful for exploring this peninsula dotted with *onsen*, though avoid lingering at the big resorts of Dōgashima, Itō or Atami itself, except to see the **MOA Museum of Art** in its extravagant setting above Atami. The MOA collection belongs to the late Okada Mokichi (1882–1955), also founder of a sect translated as 'Church of World Messianity'. A 200m (650ft) series of escalators takes you up to galleries full of Oriental ceramics, lacquer and gold, well worth the hefty admission charge. Open 09:30–16.30 Friday–Wednesday.

In central Izu, **Shuzenji Onsen** has all the usual souvenir shops, but retains a definitive old-world charm typified by vermilion bridges, which straddle the Katsura River lined with *ryokan* (Japanese inns) and bathhouses. Both the hot springs and temple are said to have been founded in 806 by the monk Kūkai. Try a dip in **Tokko-no-yu**, an open-air bath carved out of the rock. Be aware though that taking to the waters is not always fun: 800 years ago the son of Minamoto Yoritomo was supposedly poisoned here for plotting treachery.

Shimoda, where Commodore Perry arrived with his black ships in 1854 (a year after his foray into Tokyo Bay), became a treaty port after the signing of the Kanagawa Treaty at the temple of Ryōsen-ji. In 1856 **Townsend Harris** was appointed first American consul here. The Ryōsen-ji Museum has a collection of items that belonged to Harris's *geisha* (female entertainer). Open 08:30–17:00, closed 1–3 August and 26–28 December.

Nikkō National Park

Lake Chūzenji, beneath Mount Nantai, lies 10km (6.3 miles) west of Nikkō up a spectacular series of hairpin bends. It has charming cherry blossoms and autumn colours, but its most spectacular sight is the 97m (318 ft) **Kegon Falls**, which freeze in winter. The famous Tōshō-gū is in the town of Nikkō itself.

Tōshō-gū ***

It took an army of artisans over 20 years to build the Tōshō-gū, the grandiose mausoleum complex of Tokugawa Ieyasu situated among the trees of Nikkō.

From a striking pagoda, the route to the mausoleum leads through the **Nio-mon**, a gate flanked by Buddhist guardians. Next come the **Sacred Stables**, carved with a famous image of three monkeys representing the three principles of Tendai Buddhism ('hear no evil, see no evil, speak no evil').

Beyond is the **Yōmei-mon**, a Baroque structure of vermilion and gilded layers. Other buildings worth seeing are the **Honji-dō**, with its image of a 'crying dragon' on the ceiling, and the **Haiden** (Prayer Hall) and **Honden** (Main Hall). Ieyasu's tomb is up a long flight of stone steps, where there is usually some peace and quiet.

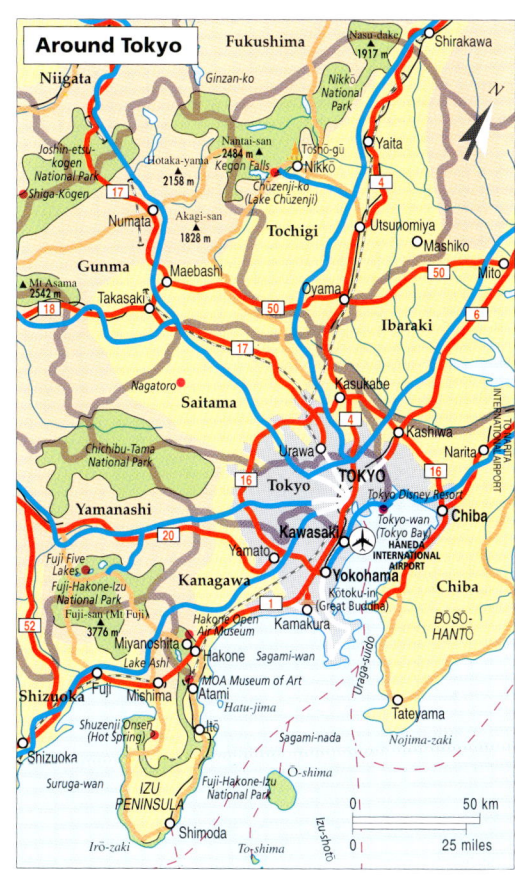

Tokyo at a Glance

BEST TIMES TO VISIT

Spring offers the most comfortable temperatures for visiting Tokyo, not to mention the bonus of cherry blossoms. **Autumn** too is pleasant, though temperatures and humidity can remain relatively high through September. Booking accommodation ahead of time is advisable during these busiest seasons and particularly if going on excursions to Nikkō or Hakone on weekends or public holidays. Note that **winter** can also be a highly attractive time for sightseeing, with cold, clear days and fewer people.

GETTING THERE

Narita International Airport is 70km (44 miles) from Tokyo. The **Airport Limousine Bus** service to the Tokyo City Air Terminal (TCAT), and other drop-off points including major hotels, is the most convenient way into central Tokyo. The **JR Narita Express** (N'EX) to Tokyo Station and Yokohama Station is fast, but expensive. The **Keisei Skyliner** rail service to Ueno is the cheapest. Taking a taxi is tantamount to bankruptcy. Domestic flights arrive at **Haneda Airport**, 20 minutes from Hamamatsu-chō by monorail, or 19 minutes by Keihin Kyūko Line from Shinagawa Station. **Tokyo Station** is the terminus for the Shinkansen route from Ōsaka and Kyoto.

GETTING AROUND

Tokyo's transport systems may appear complicated but they work efficiently. If you buy the wrong ticket by mistake you will not be penalized by Draconian measures and people are usually willing to help point you in the right direction. If in doubt about your fare, buy the cheapest ticket and pay the difference at a fare adjustment machine the other end. **Pre-paid cards** and **carnets** (*kaisūken*) are also available on most networks. **Passnet** is a travel pass covering 20 private rail and subway lines. Morning and evening rush hours peak at around 08:00 and 18:00 respectively.

Subway system: Tokyo has 12 subway lines, which are colour-coded and have signs in English. The Teito Rapid Transit Authority runs eight 'Eidan' lines: Ginza (orange), Marunouchi (red), Hibiya (grey), Tōzai (light blue), Chiyoda (green), Yūrakuchō (yellow), Hanzōmon (purple) and Namboku lines (turquoise). The Metropolitan Government runs four 'Tōei' lines: Asakusa (pale pink), Mita (dark blue), Ōedo (dark pink) and Shinjuku (light green). Eidan and Tōei lines require separate tickets but you can switch between systems with a transfer ticket, which works out cheaper. **Rail system:** JR runs the Yamanote (green), Chūō

(orange), Sōbu (yellow) and Keihin Tōhoku (blue) overground lines in Tokyo. You can buy tickets from touch-screen machines that also have displays in English. Private lines run by companies such as Tōkyū and Odakyu have their own ticket machines. JR also runs the Shinkansen lines from Tokyo and Ueno.

Buses: Buses are not the easiest way to get around owing to lack of signs in English, although Tōei buses have a flat fare of ¥200 and there is a Tōei bus guide in English. One-day passes are available for both Tōei bus and Tōei subway lines. Pay the exact fare when you board the bus.

Taxis: Stations and hotels have taxi ranks. When flagging a taxi down on the street, check that the illuminated sign is red (green means 'occupied'). The taxi driver opens and shuts passenger doors automatically. Do not interfere. Taxi fares start at ¥660 for the first 2km (1.25 miles) and rise between 23:00 and 05:00, when it can be difficult finding cabs in busy night spots such as Roppongi. Very few drivers speak any English and most are unable to navigate Tokyo very well. If you are going anywhere other than a well-known destination ask your hotel to write down the address and detailed directions, or supply a map in Japanese.

Tokyo at a Glance

Day excursions: For **Yokohama** and **Kamakura** take JR from Tokyo Station. All major Yokohama stations have tourist information centres. (The Shinkansen stops at Shin-Yokohama Station.) From Kamakura Station the Enoden Line is a picturesque route to Hase-dera and on to the island of Enoshima. There is a bicycle-hire shop next to Kamakura Station. For **Nikkō** take either the Tōbū-Nikkō Line from Asakusa Station or JR from Tokyo or Ueno via Utsunomiya (about two hours). Buy a Nikkō Mini Free Pass from Tōbu Railway (valid two days) if appropriate. For hiking maps check with the **tourist information centre** between the station and Tōshō-gū (about a 15 minute walk). **Mashiko** is an hour by bus from Utsunomiya.

WHERE TO STAY

Tokyo has literally hundreds of places to stay from the most opulent five-star hotels to cheaper business hotels and comfortable budget *ryokans* (Japanese inn) book-able through the **JNTO Welcome Inn** reservation service (*see* Travel Tips, page 124). Most hotels now have their own website with con-venient electronic booking facilities, although direct booking is not necessarily the cheapest option. Obviously, your hotel accommodation

will be included if you are on any kind of package tour.

Around the Imperial Palace
LUXURY
Capitol Tōkyū, 2-10-3 Nagatachō,Chiyoda-ku, tel: (03) 3581 4511, fax: (03) 3581 5822, website: www.tokyuhotels.co.jp Recently refurbished, the Capital is located by the Hie Shrine.

MID-RANGE
Yamanoue (Hilltop) Hotel, 1-1 Surugadai, Kanda, Chiyoda-ku, tel: (03) 3293 2311, fax: (03) 3233 4567, website: www.yamanoue-hotel.co.jp Though priced at the top-end of mid-range, this atmo-spheric Taishō-style hotel is well located.
Diamond Hotel, 25 Ichiban-chō, Chiyoda-ku, tel: (03) 3263 2211. Rather functional; in a reasonable location close to the British Embassy.

BUDGET
Sakura Hotel, 2-21-4 Jimbōchō, Kanda, Chiyoda-ku, tel: (03) 3261 3939, web-site: www.sakura-hotel.co.jp Rooms are small, but the ser-vice is *gaijin*-friendly. Handy for Kanda and central Tokyo.

Old Tokyo
MID-RANGE
Asakusa View Hotel, 3-17-1 Nishi Asakusa, Taito-ku, tel: (03) 3847 1111, fax: (03) 3842 2117. This 28-storey

hotel is the only upmarket option in Old Tokyo. It has good views and *tatami* rooms on the 6th floor.

BUDGET
Hōmeikan, 5-10-5 Hongō, Bunkyō-ku, tel: (03) 3811 1181, fax: (03) 3811 1764, website: www1.odn.ne.jp/homeikan This group of three traditional Japanese inns is off the beaten track, but provides a memorable experience.
Ryokan Asakusa Shigetsu, 1-31-11 Asakusa, Taito-ku, tel: (03) 3843 2345, fax: (03) 3843 2348, website: www.roy.hi-ho.ne.jp/shigetsu This very reasonable gem just off Nakamise-dōri is a great base for exploring Asakusa.
Sawanoya Ryokan, 2-3-11 Yanaka, Taito-ku, tel: (03) 3822 2251, fax: (03) 3822 2252. A homely, *gaijin*-friendly establishment well located for Nezu Shrine and Yanaka.

From Marunouchi to Ginza
LUXURY
Imperial Hotel, 1-1-1 Uchisaiwaichō, Chiyoda-ku, tel: (03) 3504 111, fax: (03) 3581 9146. Excellently located; long on elegant shops and short on atmosphere.
Hotel Seiyo Ginza, 1-11-2 Ginza, Chūō-ku, tel: (03) 3535 1111, fax: (03) 3535 1110, website: www.seiyo-ginza.com This designer hotel prides itself on being the last word in extravagance and efficiency.

Tokyo at a Glance

MID-RANGE
Hotel Monterey Ginza,
2-10-2 Ginza, Chūō-ku, tel:
(03) 3544 7111, fax: (03)
3544 1600. This stylish,
reasonably priced hotel is
near Ginza-itchōme Station.

BUDGET
Hotel Alcyone, Ginza, 4-14-3
Ginza, Chūō-ku, tel: (03) 3541
3621, fax: (03) 3541 3263.
Functional business hotel
near Higashi Ginza Station;
very reasonably priced.

*Tokyo Bay and South
Tokyo*
LUXURY
Le Meridien Grand Pacific,
2-6-1 Daiba, Minato-ku, tel:
(03) 5500 6711. Le Meridien
comes with an art gallery,
30th-floor restaurants and
views of Rainbow Bridge.
Takanawa Prince Hotel,
3-13-1 Takanawa, Minato-ku,
tel: (03) 3447 1111, fax: (03)
3446 0849, website: www.
princehotels.co.jp The oldest
of three Prince Hotels by
Shinagawa Station.

Cool Tokyo
LUXURY
ANA Hotel Tokyo, 1-12-33
Akasaka, Minato-ku, tel: (03)
3505 1111, fax: (03) 3505
1155, website: www.
anahotels.com A top hotel
located next to ARK Hills.
Hotel Ōkura, 2-10-4
Toranomon, Minato-ku,
tel: (03) 3582 0111, fax: (03)
3582 3707, website: www.

okura.com The Ōkura is the
grande dame of Tokyo's top
hotels, convenient for
Roppongi and Akasaka.
Hotel New Ōtani, 4-1
Kioi-chō, Chiyoda-ku, tel: (03)
3265 1111, fax: (03) 3221
2619, website: www.
newotanihotels.com Known
for its charming Japanese
garden and expensive La Tour
d'Argent restaurant.
The Westin Tokyo, 1-4-1
Mita, Meguro-ku, tel: (03)
5423 7000, fax: (03) 5423
7600, website: www.
westin.co.jp This sumptuous
European-style hotel is right
behind Ebisu Garden Place.

MID-RANGE
Roppongi Prince Hotel,
3-2-7 Roppongi, Minato-ku,
tel: (03) 3587 1111, fax: (03)
3587 0770. Built around a
pool, this hotel is conveniently
situated and mildly stylish.
Hotel Ibis, 7-14-4 Roppongi,
Minato-ku, tel: (03) 3403
4411, fax: (03) 3479 0609.
In the thick of the action by
Roppongi Crossing. Func-
tional and reasonably priced.
Hotel Excellent, 1-9-5 Ebisu-
nishi, Shibuya-ku, tel: (03)
5458 0087, fax: (03) 5458
8787. If The Westin is but a
pipe dream, try this popular
business hotel in Ebisu.

BUDGET
Asia Centre of Japan,
8-10-32 Akasaka, Minato-ku,
tel: (03) 3402 6111, fax: (03)
3402 0738. Well located near

Nogizaka Station. Tiny rooms
reflect the budget price.

*From Shinjuku to
Ikebukurō*
LUXURY
Park Hyatt, 3-7-1-2
Nishi-Shinjuku, Shinjuku-ku,
tel: (03) 5322 1234, fax: (03)
5322 1288, website: www.
parkhyatttokyo.com Easily
the most luxurious skyscraper
accommodation in Tokyo.
Four Seasons at Chinzansō,
2-10-8 Sekiguchi, Bunkyō-ku,
tel: (03) 3943 2222, fax: (03)
3943 2300, website: www.
fourseasons-tokyo.com/tokyo
Far from the madding
crowds, with a beautiful
garden setting.

MID-RANGE
**Shinjuku Washington
Hotel**, 3-2-9 Nishi-Shinjuku,
Shinjuku-ku, tel: (03) 3343
3111, fax: (03) 3342 2575.
An unimaginative but much
cheaper alternative to
Shinjuku's luxury hotels.

BUDGET
Hotel Tateshina, 5-8-6
Shinjuku, Shinjuku-ku, tel:
(03) 3350 5271, fax: (03)
3350 5275, website:
tateshina.co.jp Small
rooms, but well located
for Shinjuku Gyoen.
Kimi Ryokan, 2-36-8
Ikebukuro, Toshima-ku (west
station exit), tel: (03) 3971
3766, website: www.
kimiwillbe.com (website is
an information centre for for-

Tokyo at a Glance

eigners.) Tokyo's top budget hang-out for travellers.

Around Tokyo: Nikkō
LUXURY
Nikkō Kanaya Hotel, 1300 Kamihatsuishi-machi, Nikkō City, Tochigi Prefecture, tel: (0288) 54 0001, fax: (0288) 53 2487, website: www.kanayahotel.co.jp Much more expensive than in Isabella Bird's day, but still a great institution.

BUDGET
Turtle Inn, 2-16 Takumi-chō, Nikkō City, tel: (0288) 53 3168, fax: (0288) 53 3883. Good location. Western- or Japanese-style rooms. Meals on request.

WHERE TO EAT
Tokyo
From fast-food venues to elegant extravaganzas of traditional Japanese fare costing over ¥10,000 per person, Tokyo has an unbelievable range of restaurants. Department stores, hotels and shopping malls are crammed with eateries. See www.bento.com for a comprehensive range of over 1000 restaurant reviews. Useful chains to know include **Monsoon** (Modern Asian) **Moti** (Indian), **Sushisei** (sushi) and **Anna Miller's** (pure American comfort with free coffee refills). Reservations are advised where phone numbers are given. If you find

yourself in a local Japanese restaurant with no English menu, set some kind of price limit and say to the proprietor: 'o makase shimasu' which means, 'I'll leave it up to you'.

Around the Imperial Palace
LUXURY
Kandagawa Honten, 2-5-11 Soto-Kanda, Chiyoda-ku, tel: (03) 3251 5031. An old Japanese restaurant offering some of the best unagi (eel) in town. Closed Sundays.

MID-RANGE
All major hotels such as the **Capitol Tōkyū** have a range of restaurants and coffee shops. The Kanda area has a wide array of coffee shops. **Tohryū**, 4-2-2 Kōjimachi, Chiyoda-ku. Branches of this tasty Chinese restaurant are also at the World Trade Centre, Hamamatsuchō, and Azabu Jūban. **Champ de Soleil**, 1-10-6 Uchi-Kanda, Chiyoda-ku. Belgian bistro mussels, frites and beer. Closed Sundays.

BUDGET
Miro, 2-4-6 Kanda Surugadai, Chiyoda-ku (alley behind the Pachinko parlour opposite JR Ochanomizu Station). Atmospheric 1950s-style café with works by Miro.

Old Tokyo
MID-RANGE
Hantei, 2-12-15 Nezu, Bunkyo-ku, tel: (03) 3828

1440. Kushi-age (food on skewers) cuisine in an old wooden setting. Courses come in batches of six. Closed Mondays.
Kawasaki, 2-13-1 Ryōgoku Sumida-ku, tel (03) 3631 2529. Long-standing chanko Nabe restaurant (see page 27) in sumō land. Closed on Sundays.
Sumidagawa Brewery Pub, 1-23-36 Azumabashi, 3rd floor, Sumida-ku. By the Philippe Starck 'Golden Flame', this pub offers a wide range of beers and Japanese fare.

BUDGET
Kamiya Bar,1-1-1 Asakusa, Taito-ku. A 200-year-old bar to try for the atmosphere.

From Marunouchi to Ginza
LUXURY
Daidaiya, 8-5 Ginza Nine Building No. 1, tel: (03) 5537 3566. A glitzy Asian fusion dining experience with branches also in Akasaka and Shinjuku.
Robata, 1-3-8 Yūrakuchō, Chiyoda-ku (close to the Imperial Hotel along JR tracks). Authentic, country-style cooking in a rickety building with dark wooden counters. No English menu.
Ten-ichi, 6-6-5 Ginza, Chūō-ku, tel: (03) 3571 1949. Simply the best tempura in town. Branches also in the Sony Building, the Imperial Hotel and the Mitsui Building in Nishi-Shinjuku.

Tokyo at a Glance

MID-RANGE

The new **Marunouchi Building**, 2-4-1 Marunouchi, Chiyoda-ku (near Tokyo Post Office) has a superb range of restaurants including, on the 5th floor, **West Park Café Marunouchi** (Californian deli) and **Papaya Leaf** (Oriental fusion); on the 35th floor **Mango Tree Tokyo** (good Thai), and **Aux Amis Tokyo** (French wine bar), and on the 36th floor, **Antica Osteria del Ponte** (Italian).

BUDGET

Tsukiji Market, fresh sushi breakfast in the barrack buildings in front of the market. **Yūrakuchō**, cheap *yakitori* (skewered food) stalls under the JR lines at Yūraku-chō Station.

Tokyo Bay and South Tokyo
MID-RANGE

Decks Tokyo Beach, Island Mall, 1-6-1 Daiba, Minato-ku, is a pleasant place for a drink while **Little Hong Kong** (6th and 7th floor of Decks) has good Chinese restaurants. Try **Tenten Tsunetsune Kaitenbō** (7th floor) for conveyor-belt *dim sum*. **Monsoon Café**, Daiba 1-7-1, Mediage 4th floor (Aquacity). Part of the Monsoon group. Southeast Asian cuisine. Open late. **Aguri**, 1-6-7 Kami-Meguro, Kajima Building, 1st floor, Meguro-ku. A user-friendly

izakaya, with a wide range of dishes and sake.

BUDGET

Tonki, 1-1-2 Shimo-Meguro, Meguro-ku (by Meguro Station). Tokyo's most famous *tonkatsu* establishment. Queues move fairly quickly. Closed Tuesdays.

Cool Tokyo
LUXURY

Gesshinkyo, 4-24-12 Jingumae, Shibuya-ku (off Omotesandō-dōri), tel: (03) 3796 6575. Exquisite *shōjin ryōri* (vegetarian cuisine). Reservations obligatory. **Fukuzushi**, 5-7-8 Roppongi, Minato-ku (behind Hard Rock Café), tel: (03) 3402 4116. Stylish, delicious and expensive sushi. Closed Sundays.

MID-RANGE

Chibo, 38F Ebisu Garden Place Tower, 4-20-30 Ebisu, Shibuya-ku. Okonomiyaki at reasonable prices with great views. More restaurants on 38F/39F. **Irreel**, 3-29-16 Ebisu, ABC Annex Building 3F (opposite Sapporo Brewery HQ), tel: (03) 5475 6127. An intimate, excellent taste of Paris in Tokyo. Closed Tuesdays. **Vision Network/Las Chicas**, 5-47-6 Jingumae, Shibuya-ku (off Aoyama-dōri near Omotesandō Station), tel: (03) 3407 6865 (for outside table in summer). Pacific rim cuisine, casual, *gaijin*-friendly.

Lunchan Bar & Grill, Alive Mitake Building, 1st floor, 1-2-5 Shibuya, Shibuya-ku (off Aoyama-dōri behind Kodomo no Shiro), tel: (03) 5466 1398 (for Sunday brunch reservations). Californian-style cuisine with good wines. **Nambantei**, 4-5-6 Roppongi, tel: (03) 3402 0606. *Gaijin*-friendly *yakitori-ya*. Set courses not too expensive.

BUDGET

Crayon House, 3-8-15 Kita Aoyama, Minato-ku (turn at Hanae Mori Building off Omotesandō-dōri). Two healthfood restaurants: '**Hiroba**' (Japanese) and '**Home**' (French). **Lion Café**, 2-19-13 Dōgenzaka, Shibuya-ku (past Tōhō Cinema, turn right at Yachiyo Bank. Look for a yellow, white and green sign with a lion). A unique experience of classical music to coffee.

From Shinjuku to Ikebukuro
LUXURY

New York Grill, 52F Park Hyatt Hotel (*see* Where To Stay, page 118), tel: (03) 5323 3458. Expensive, unforgettable American dining experience high up above Tokyo.

MID-RANGE

The **Sunshine City** complex in Ikebukuro has numerous restaurants.

Tokyo at a Glance

Parc Café, 1-1-1 Shinjuku, Shinjuku-ku, tel: (03) 3350 5445. A good French bistro with a view of Shinjuku Gyoen.
Tsunahachi, 3-31-8, Shinjuku, Shinjuku-ku, tel: (03) 3352 1012. Great tempura in a traditional building with *shitamachi* style.
Nakamura, Shimokitazawa MT Building 2nd floor, 2-37-3 Kitazawa, Setagaya-ku, tel: (03) 3466 4020. Cool, contemporary Japanese cuisine with over 20 kinds of sake. No English menu, so set a price and let the staff choose.
Eat a Peach/Trouble Peach, 2-9-16 Kitazawa, Setagaya-ku, tel: (03) 3460 1468. Trouble Peach (upstairs) is a funky bar of minute proportions with a huge record collection.

Yokohama
MID-RANGE
Yokohama Station mall, MM21 and Chinatown all have a huge choice.
Yamate-jūbankan, 247 Yamate-chō. French cuisine, snacks and a beer garden in summer up on the Bluff.

Kamakura
The Komachi-dōri area has plenty of inexpensive Japanese restaurants.
Hachi-no-ki, 7 Yamanouchi, Kamakura City (by Kenchō-ji), tel: (0467) 22 8719. First-class *shōjin-ryōri* (vegetarian cuisine). Closed Mondays. Two other branches near Tōkei-ji.

SHOPPING
American Pharmacy, Hibiya Park Building, 1-8-1 Yūraku-chō. English-speaking pharmacists.
Japan Traditional Crafts Centre, Plaza 246 Building, opposite Bell Commons, Aoyama-dōri.
Kinokuniya Bookstore, Takashimaya Times Square Annexe, Shinjuku. Huge foreign-language book selection.
Maruzen, in Nihombashi. Another good bookstore.
Oriental Bazaar, 5-9-13 Jingū-mae (half way down Omotesandō). Ideal for gifts, from kimonos to ceramics. Closed Thursdays.

TOURS AND EXCURSIONS
Japan Travel Bureau, tel: (03) 5620 9500. *Sunrise Tours* with English-speaking guide in Tokyo. Also Kamakura, Tokyo DisneyLand etc.
Japan Gray Line Company, tel: (03) 3433 5745. Half- or full-day tours of Tokyo by bus.
Walking tours can be arranged with volunteers. Check with JNTO.

USEFUL CONTACTS
JNTO Tourist Information Centre, 10 Fl., Tokyo Kōtsu Kaikan Building, 2-10-1 Yūrakuchō, Chiyoda-ku, Tokyo 100-0006, tel: (03) 3201 3331. Open 09:00–17:00 Monday–Friday, 09:00–12:00 Saturdays. Also handles **Welcome Inn** reservations, tel: (03) 3211 4201, fax: (03) 3211 9009.
Narita International Airport (main office in Terminal 2, branch office in Terminal 1) tel: (0476) 34 6251. Open 09:00–20:00.
American Express, tel: (0120) 02 0120.
Teletourist Service, tel: (03) 3201 2911. For 24-hour taped information in English on Tokyo events.
Ticket Pia, tel: (03) 5237 9966. English-language telephone booking for sports, concerts, theatre etc.
Tokyo Medical Information Service, tel: (03) 5285 8181. Helps locate medical services. For emergency interpreting tel: (03) 5285 8185.

Tokyo Medical Clinic, 32 Mori Building, 3-4-30 Shiba Kōen, Minato-ku, tel: (03) 3436 3028. Appointments with English-speaking doctors.
Useful Publications: The *Tokyo Weekender* is free at various hotels and bars. The Saturday edition of *The Japan Times* is particularly useful for exhibition and theatre listings. The monthly *Tokyo Journal* (also online at www.tokyo.to) has useful features and reviews, while Metropolis at www.metropolis.co.jp has some excellent features and reviews.
Tokyo Q's website www.tokyoq.com tells you what is on and also carries restaurant reviews.

Travel Tips

Tourist Information

The **Japan National Tourist Organization** (**JNTO**) is the best source of information. The JNTO website has excellent information: www.jnto.go.jp

Main overseas offices:

UK: Heathcoat House, 20 Savile Row, London W1S 3PR, tel: (020) 7734 9638, fax: (020) 7734 4290.

USA: One Rockefeller Plaza, Suite 1250, New York, NY 10020, tel: (212) 757 5640, fax: (212) 307 6754.

Other offices: Bangkok, Beijing, Chicago, Frankfurt, Hong Kong, Los Angeles, Paris, San Francisco, Seoul, Sydney, Toronto.

For English-speaking staff and a huge range of maps/leaflets go to the **JNTO Tourist Information Centre** (**TIC**), 10 Fl., Tokyo Kōtsu Kaikan Building, 2-10-1 Yūrakuchō, Chiyoda-ku, Tokyo 100-0006, tel: (03) 3201 3331. Open 09:00–17:00 Mon–Fri; 09:00–12:00 Sat, closed on national holidays and 29 Dec–3 Jan.

Narita International Airport also has a **TIC** (main office in Terminal 2, branch office in Terminal 1), tel: (0476) 34 6251. Open 09:00–20.00. On day excursions outside Tokyo, note that there are also Information Centres at the following railway stations: Shin-Yokohama, Sakuraguichō (Yokohama), Kamakura and Nikkō Tōbu. The sign to look for is marked with a question mark and the word 'information'.

Entry Requirements

Japan has reciprocal visa exemption arrangements with over 60 countries including the UK, Canada, Republic of Ireland, USA and New Zealand. Citizens of these countries entering Japan for tourist or business purposes can stay for **90 days without a visa** (up to 6 months in the case of the UK and Ireland). Citizens of **South Africa** need tourist visas. For visa information, check the Ministry of Foreign Affairs website **www.mofa.go.jp** or ask your local Japanese embassy. If spending more than 90 days in Japan, all foreigners must register and carry an Alien Registration Card.

Customs

The **duty free allowance** for **non-residents** (over 20 years) is 400 cigarettes or 250g of tobacco (or a 500g combination), three 750ml bottles of alcohol and 57g (2oz) of perfume, plus up to ¥200,000 of gifts and souvenirs. Any amount of currency may be brought into the country. Prohibited items include firearms and pornographic material. **Illegal drugs** are not tolerated, as Paul McCartney once found to his cost; jail is not part of any recommended itinerary in Japan. Quarantine regulations ban the import of plants, fresh fruits, raw meat etc.

Health Requirements

There are no special health or vaccination requirements for entering Japan.

Getting There

By Air: A range of European, US and Asian airlines all fly daily to **Narita International Airport** (including Eva Air). Narita is 70km (44 miles) from Tokyo. **Haneda Airport** now operates domestic flights only. (See 'At a Glance' page 116 for the best routes into the city).

By Rail: If arriving in Tokyo from China, Russia or Korea by ferry to Fukuoka, Ōsaka or Kōbe, or from Kansai International Airport, Shinkansen (bullet trains) and other trains arrive at Tokyo Station.

What to Pack

Plenty of changes of **light cotton** clothing and an umbrella are essential in summer, when Tokyo sweats with humidity. **Comfortable clothes for sitting on** *tatami* are also important. A mixture of layers (including a coat in winter) is useful to cater both for over-air-conditioned and over-heated buildings and trains. The Japanese tend to dress smartly (whether formal or casual). Err on the side of caution at classy restaurants or hotels. **Slip-on shoes** are very useful, as temples, shrines, *tatami* rooms and ordinary homes are shoe-free zones. Hole-free socks avoid toe-curling embarrassment in traditional restaurants or *ryokan*. Rail stations have many flights of steps and there is virtually no space on trains for big suitcases, so try to pack lightly if you plan to travel a lot.

Money Matters

Currency: The yen comes in ¥1, ¥5, ¥10, ¥50, ¥100 and ¥500 coins and in ¥1000, ¥2000, ¥5000 and ¥10,000 notes.
Exchange: Japan's banking system is cumbersome. **Cash**

is king. Keep the yen equivalent of several hundred dollars or pounds on you. The low crime rate means this is not as crazy as it sounds. **American Express** and **Visa** are the most widely accepted credit cards. **Traveller's cheques** can be exchanged at all major banks (open 09:00–15:00 Mon–Fri; foreign exchange desks do not always open at 09:00), but be prepared to wait. Most **Post Offices** (09:00–17:00 Mon–Fri) and big hotels will change major currencies. Japanese **ATMs** generally accept only Japanese-issued cards (read notices carefully). **Citibank ATMs** (open 24 hours) will give cash advances on foreign-issued cards.
Tipping: This is an alien concept in Japan. Service charges are usually incorporated in the bill. Do not tip taxi drivers, and restaurant or hotel staff.
Consumption Tax: A five per cent tax is charged on all goods and services, sometimes inclusive of the quoted price and sometimes exclusive. A local tax of three per cent is added to hotel bills

over ¥15,000 per night and over ¥7,500 per person in restaurants. This may make it cheaper not to charge all meals to your room bill.

Accommodation:

Western-style accommodation is normally charged on a **room-only** basis. **Japanese-style** accommodation is on a **per-person basis** and includes breakfast and dinner. **Luxury:** (¥25,000 upwards). A night in a top *ryokan* (Japanese inn) with *kaiseki ryōri* in **tatami** rooms (sleeping 2–4 people) and a beautiful garden setting can cost ¥40,000 per person or more. Any *ryokan* will have communal baths for men and women, which is all part of the experience. **Top Western-style hotels** costing ¥25,000 plus per night or more offer all first-class amenities.
Mid-range: (¥10–25,000). Second tier *ryokan* range from around ¥12,000–¥20,000 (or more) for an *en-suite* room.
Business hotels offer a solid, if sometimes soulless Western option for the independent traveller. Generally reliable

CONVERSION CHART		
FROM	**TO**	**MULTIPLY BY**
Millimetres	Inches	0.0394
Metres	Yards	1.0936
Metres	Feet	3.281
Kilometres	Miles	0.6214
Square kilometres	Square miles	0.386
Hectares	Acres	2.471
Litres	Pints	1.760
Kilograms	Pounds	2.205
Tonnes	Tons	0.984
To convert Celsius to Fahrenheit: x 9 ÷ 5 + 32		

chains include the **Daiichi, Tōkyū** and **Washington** groups. **Budget:** (Under ¥10,000 per person). *Ryokan* in this price range (some have a no-meal option) provide perfectly good accommodation. **Capsule hotels**, have coffin-like rooms with all amenities; they are not for the claustrophobic, and rarely used by women. If you are completely stuck, **love hotels** can be good value for an overnight stay (not their intended purpose). **Cheaper business hotels** usually provide *yukata*, toothbrush and shampoo. **Reservations:** reserve well ahead particularly at weekends and public holidays such as New Year, Golden Week (first week of May), August and in spring and autumn.

PUBLIC HOLIDAYS

1 January • New Year
2nd Mon of January
• Coming-of-Age Day
11 February
• National Foundation Day
Around 21 March
• Vernal Equinox
29 April • Greenery Day
3 May
• Constitution Memorial Day
5 May • Children's Day
20 July • Marine Day
15 September
• Respect-for-the-Aged Day
Around 23 September
• Autumnal Equinox
2nd Mon of October
• Sports Day
3 November • Culture Day
23 November
• Labour Thanksgiving Day
23 December
• Emperor's Birthday

Top hotels have English-speaking staff and most have websites, which allow you to make reservations by email. For cheaper hotels, try the Japan City Hotel Association at www.jcha.or.jp JNTO's Welcome Reservation Centre offers reservation services from overseas via the web at www.itcj.or.jp for budget accommodation. JNTO's own website www.jnto.go.jp also offers links to reservation services.

Eating Out

Tokyo boasts an astonishing array of international cuisine from Indian and Italian to Thai and Mexican. You will rarely be short of a pizza if raw fish is not your thing. The most comprehensive on-line food guide covering over 1000 establishments is www. bento.com The Japanese eat early: lunch runs from 11:30 and dinner from 18:00. If you cannot stomach the idea of a Japanese breakfast (rice, raw egg, seaweed and fish), try a coffee shop for *mōningu sābisu* (usually an egg, toast and coffee). The **teishoku** (a set meal of 2–3 dishes, miso soup and rice) is the non-Japanese speaker's godsend. Here is a guide to some eating and drinking establishments:
izakaya – informal, noisy restaurants serving range of dishes such as *yakitori*.
aka-chōchin – type of *izakaya* with red lanterns outside.
kissaten – coffee shop usually serving *mōningu setto* breakfast (toast, egg, coffee) and other simple meals.

nomiya – bar with counter; regulars keep their own bottles.
robataya – serves rustic-style charcoal-grilled food (the preparation of which is often a theatrical performance).
ryōtei – elegant, expensive restaurant serving *kaiseki ryōri*
shokudō – convenient, inexpensive. Order from plastic food models in the window.
sushiya – sit at the counter and choose your sushi or order a *teishoku*. *Kaiten-zushi* is sushi on a conveyor belt. Price is determined by the colour of the plate.
yatai – outdoor stalls cooking simple dishes. Can be good.

Transport

Rail: Japan's rail system is the best in the world. Japan Rail (JR) runs six major regional networks. Private companies operate several others. If you are planning at least one return journey beyond Tokyo (to Kyoto, for example) buy a **Japan Rail Pass** from JAL (if flying JAL), JTB or other agents *before you leave for Japan*. An exchange voucher for a one-, two- or three-week JR Pass for ordinary or Green Car (first class) use can only be purchased **outside Japan by temporary visitors**. On arrival, exchange the voucher at a JR Travel Service Centre. The JR Pass is valid on all JR trains except the *Nozomi* (Super-Express) Shinkansen. You can also use it on all JR lines within Tokyo (such as the Yamanote Line) and on journeys by JR to Yokohama, Kamakura and Nikkō etc. See www.japanrailpass.net

for full details. On journeys outside Tokyo, Rail Pass holders can make **seat reservations** at no extra cost. This makes sense at busy periods or to ensure a non-smoking seat. English timetables, available from JNTO, provide adequate reference for most routes. Go to the **midori no madoguchi** (Green Window Counter) at any rail station with the number of the train you want to catch, date and destination (preferably written down). Station luggage lockers are handy for lightening your load, but can only be used for up to three days. The **JR East Infoline**, tel: (03) 3423 0111, open 10:00–18.00 Mon–Fri, is an English-language information service for nationwide train enquiries. **Shinkansen** (bullet trains) operate on six different lines. The *Kodama* stops at all Tōkaidō line stations; the *Hikari* at major stations and the *Nozomi* (reserved seats only) only seven times between Tokyo and Hakata (Kyūshū), a journey of around five hours. Individual tickets are subject to a Shinkansen surcharge. **Tokkyū** (limited express trains) also require a surcharge but seats can be reserved. **Kaisoku** (rapid trains) have no surcharge. **Futsū** (ordinary trains) stop at every station.

Car hire: It is best to leave Tokyo by train, but hire a car if you are going to the Izu Peninsula or off the beaten track. Keep the cost down by avoiding expressways (tolls are

exorbitant). Use Shōbunsha's bilingual *Japan Road Atlas*. Japan drives on the left and road signs are in both *kanji* and Roman letters. The top speed limit is 100kph (62.5mph) on expressways and 80kph (50mph) on metropolitan highways. To hire a car you need an International Driver's Licence and your own national licence. Cars can be rented at airports and stations from most internationally known operators. **Eki (Station) Rent-a-car** has good deals combining train and car hire for excursions.

Business Hours

Shops are open from around 10:00–20:00, including Sundays. Most close one day a week. Convenience Stores such as Seven Eleven operate 24 hours. **Museums tend to close on Mondays and New Year**. If a public holiday falls on a Monday, many shut the following day instead. Note that the smaller museums may close in the few days before a new exhibition. Always check local listings before making a special trip. **Last admission is usually 30 minutes before closing time**.

Time Difference

Japan is 9 hours ahead of Greenwich Mean Time (GMT).

Communications

Telephone services in Japan are expensive, but getting cheaper. Pre-paid phone cards (*terefon kādo*) for public telephones can be bought from vending machines or

newspaper kiosks. Cards valid for international calls (*kokusai denwa*) come in ¥1000, ¥3000 and ¥5000 units and can be used in grey pay phones marked 'international' or 'ISDN'. **Fax** facilities are available at top hotels, post offices and convenience stores. **Public Internet access** is becoming a more widely understood concept, so checking email is getting easier. At a price, access is possible at Kinko's business stores and at a growing number of cybercafés. For buying a cell phone *see* page 24.

Electricity

Japan operates on a 100V current. Plugs are of the flat, two-pin variety. A transformer must be used for overseas appliances.

Weights and Measures

Japan uses the metric system, though retains some quirks of its own like the *tsubo* (3.954 sq yards), to measure space.

Health Precautions

Tap water is safe to drink, if not very palatable. Despite past outbreaks of *E. coli* food poisoning, Japan is generally a safe place to eat. Mosquitoes can be a nuisance in summer, but successfully combated with mosquito coils. Malaria is not an issue. A comparatively high percentage of Japanese are carriers of Hepatitis B, which is more of a problem than HIV. Fortunately, Japan is a condom-friendly society. The contraceptive pill has finally been given approval, but bring your own.

Personal Safety

The crime rate in Tokyo is remarkably low. You are more likely to have a lost item returned to you than have anything stolen. However, take all sensible precautions. The incidence of rape is low (probably under-reported). In general, it is safe for women to walk on their own at night. The most common complaint

is 'groping' on crowded commuter trains; a stamp on the foot combined with verbal abuse can work wonders.

Emergencies

The emergency service telephone number for an **ambulance** or the **fire brigade** is 119. For the **police**, it is 110, but do not expect assistance in English. In an emergency try the toll-free 24 hour **English-speaking Japan Helpline**, tel: (0120) 461 997.

Etiquette

The Japanese will forgive you just about anything for being foreign, but some basic rules will help avoid real faux pas.
• Take a name or business card with you. This is a certificate of existence. Treat business cards from others with respect. (Do not doodle on them.)
• The Japanese give their surname first (as does this book). It is polite to always add *San* to a name, e.g. Suzuki *San* (Mr or Mrs, or Miss Suzuki).
• Always be prepared to remove your shoes.
• Stay cool under trying circumstances. Losing your temper gets you nowhere.

GOOD READING

Bird, **Isabella** (1984) *Unbeaten Tracks in Japan*, Virago.
Bix, **Herbert** (2000) *Hirohito and the Makings of Modern Japan*, HarperCollins.
Crowell, **Todd** (2002) *Tokyo: City on the Edge*, Asia 2000.
Hearn, **Lafcadio** (1984) *Writings from Japan*, Penguin.
Kerr, **Alex** (2001) *Dogs and Demons*, Hill and Wang.
Schilling, **Mark** (1997) *Encyclopaedia of Japanese Pop Culture*, Weatherhill.
Seidensticker, **Edward** (1983) *Low City, High City*, Tuttle.